A READER'S DIGEST SONGBOOK

REMEMBERING THE '50s

Editor: William L. Simon
Music arranged and edited by Dan Fox
Senior Staff Editor: Mary Kelleher
Designer: Judy Speicher
Staff Editor: Eileen Hughes
Editorial Assistant: Mark Pengelski
Annotations by Richard M. Sudhalter
Illustrations by Nancy Stahl and Heidi Younger
Music Associate: Elizabeth Mead
Rights Manager: Lisa Garrett Smith

READER'S DIGEST GENERAL BOOKS
Editor in Chief: John A. Pope, Jr.
Managing Editor: Jane Polley
Executive Editor: Susan J. Wernert
Art Director: David Trooper
Group Editors: Will Bradbury, Sally French, Norman B. Mack, Kaari Ward
Group Art Editors: Evelyn Bauer, Robert M. Grant, Joel Musler
Chief of Research: Laurel A. Gilbride
Copy Chief: Edward W. Atkinson
Picture Editor: Richard Pasqual
Rights and Permissions: Pat Colomban
Head Librarian: Jo Manning

THE READER'S DIGEST ASSOCIATION, INC.
Pleasantville, New York/Montreal

Reader's Digest Fund for the Blind is publisher of the Large-Type Edition of *Reader's Digest.* For subscription information about this magazine, please contact Reader's Digest Fund for the Blind, Inc., Dept. 250, Pleasantville, N.Y. 10570.

Remembering the '50s
100 Top Hits to Play and Sing

INDEX TO SECTIONS

Section 1: The New "Standard" Hits of the '50s 4
Section 2: Old Hits Made New in the '50s 49
Section 3: Hit Songs from Hit Shows 77
Section 4: The Big Film Songs 113
Section 5: Hits from Faraway Places 153

Section 6: Elvis and the Rock Revolution 173
Section 7: Country-Style Crossover Hits 212
Section 8: Ballads with a Beat 231
Section 9: Folk-Style Hits of the '50s 258

INDEX TO SONGS

All the Way 126
Answer Me, My Love 166
Any Time 220
Around the World 142
Arrivederci, Roma 153
Autumn Leaves 168
Baubles, Bangles and Beads 77
Blossom Fell, A 6
Blue Velvet 231
Blueberry Hill 59
Bye Bye, Love 200
Catch a Falling Star 22
Charlie Brown 203
Cold, Cold Heart 228
Cry 14
Crying in the Chapel 224
Don't Be Cruel (to a Heart That's True) ...187
Earth Angel 249
Enjoy Yourself (It's Later Than You Think) ...27
Fascination 72
Gigi 129
Goodnight, Irene 264
Great Balls of Fire 209
Great Pretender, The 240
Hawaiian Wedding Song, The 19
Hello, Young Lovers 83
He's Got the Whole World in His Hands ...270
Hi-Lili, Hi-Lo 132
Hound Dog 176
I Almost Lost My Mind 218
I Apologize 67
I Believe 40
I Could Have Danced All Night 106
I Get Ideas 170
I Want You, I Need You, I Love You 178
I Whistle a Happy Tune 86
If You Love Me (Really Love Me) 162
I'll Never Stop Loving You 147
I'm Walking Behind You 32
In the Cool, Cool, Cool of the Evening 150
It Isn't Fair 64
It's All in the Game 74
I've Never Been in Love Before 100
Jailhouse Rock 190
Just in Time 94
Kisses Sweeter Than Wine 268
La Bamba 192
Love Is a Many-Splendored Thing 113
Love Letters in the Sand 62
Love Me Tender 182
Loveliest Night of the Year, The 144

Mack the Knife 92
Man That Got Away, The 137
Mary Anne 266
Melody of Love 54
Mr. Wonderful 102
Misty 24
Moments to Remember 8
My Prayer 56
My Special Angel 246
Naughty Lady of Shady Lane, The 16
Nel Blu, Dipinto di Blu (Volare) 156
Night Train 206
Oh! My Papa 160
Old Piano Roll Blues, The 30
On the Street Where You Live 110
On Top of Old Smokey 263
Only You 234
Peggy Sue 195
P.S. I Love You 70
Put Your Head on My Shoulder 255
Que Será, Será (Whatever Will Be, Will Be) ...124
Rock Around the Clock 198
Secret Love 116
Seventy-Six Trombones 96
Shake, Rattle and Roll 173
Sincerely 252
Sound of Music, The 89
Stranger in Paradise 80
(Let Me Be Your) Teddy Bear 184
Tell Me Why 11
Tennessee Waltz 222
That's Amore 134
Three Coins in the Fountain 121
Till 35
Till I Waltz Again with You 46
Tom Dooley 258
Too Young 38
Twelfth of Never, The 260
Unchained Melody 118
Unforgettable 4
Vaya con Dios 43
Volare (Nel Blu, Dipinto di Blu) 156
What a Diff'rence a Day Made 49
Whatever Will Be, Will Be (Que Será, Será) ...124
Wheel of Fortune 243
Who's Sorry Now? 52
Why Don't You Believe Me 237
Yellow Bird 274
Yellow Rose of Texas, The 272
You Don't Know Me 215
Your Cheatin' Heart 212

Introduction

"So tell me, Grandpa, what was it really like to grow up in the '50s?"

Drifting with varying degrees of resistance into middle age, a whole generation finds itself facing that innocuous little question. In answering it, many a once-upon-a-time prom queen or BMOC (that's Big Man on Campus, for those who weren't around then) has made a startling discovery: there are actually *two* versions of growing up in the '50s.

One—fed by TV, movies and the other pop culture trappings—would have us believe that it was all a real-life storyboard for *Happy Days*: hot rods, leather jackets and duck-tail haircuts, "Hound Dog" and "Shake, Rattle and Roll." No nerds need apply. That's how it was; right, Gramps?

Well, yes and no. Another version of the '50s, marching alongside the *Happy Days* scenario like the parallel universe in a sci-fi short story, takes a more sober-sided view. World War II wasn't long over, and already we were involved in another war, this time in Korea; Sen. Joseph R. McCarthy was finding Communists in the unlikeliest of places; and otherwise reasonable people were building atomic bomb shelters in their basements.

According to this scenario, the '50s were a time when you grew up fast, got married young and took on responsibility the minute you walked off the campus. No wonder that the photos of seniors in mid-'50s yearbooks look so much older than today's counterparts do.

Now have a look at the following pages, at the songs we sang and listened to in those complex years. Did the same decade really produce Nat King Cole singing "They tried to tell us we're too young," *and* Bill Haley urging everyone to "Rock around the clock"?

Sure did. It's almost as if the two images were united in one common philosophy: Have a ball tonight, because tomorrow—or in a year or an hour from now—you may have to grow up awfully fast.

In the meantime, we had romance ("Love Is a Many-Splendored Thing"), heartbreak ("Blue Velvet"), country sentiment ("Your Cheatin' Heart"), stoic acceptance ("Que Será, Será") and nostalgia ("The Old Piano Roll Blues"). We had our own oldies ("P.S. I Love You"), songs of faith and inspiration ("I Believe"), folk favorites ("Tom Dooley") and Broadway hits ("On the Street Where You Live").

And, yes, we indeed had rock and roll; and, yes, it did cause something of a revolution. When Elvis appeared on *The Ed Sullivan Show* he was shown only from the waist up, so as not to incite either undue hormonal activity or righteous indignation, depending on who was watching. The countless thousands of teenagers on whom the Fonz was modeled were indeed central players in this part of the drama. When Jerry Lee Lewis pounded out "Great Balls of Fire," Jimmy Forrest honked his way through "Night Train" and Elvis hip-swiveled through "Jailhouse Rock," it was nothing short of insurrection.

But it wasn't the whole story. Not by a long shot. Just part of a decade that, viewed in retrospect, was one of the most complicated, varied and challenging in the history of our century. And the music on the following pages brings it all back.

What was it like growing up in the '50s? Hey, you can dig it. Just sit down at the piano, turn the page and start playing and singing. The music will tell the rest of the story in its own amazing and utterly irrepressible way.

How to Use This Book

As in all Reader's Digest music books, the arrangements in *Remembering the '50s* were designed to be easy to play while still being musically interesting and artistically gratifying. For vocalists and players of any treble clef instruments, the melody is on top, clear and uncluttered, with the stems of the notes turned up. However, if one plays in tandem with a piano or organ, it must be on a "C" instrument, such as a violin, flute, recorder, oboe, accordion, harmonica, melodica or an electronic keyboard. Guitarists can also play the melody as written, or they can play chords from the symbols (G7, Am, etc.) or from the diagrams printed just above the staves. Organists whose instruments have foot pedals may use the *small* pedal notes in the bass clef (with stems turned down). *But these pedal notes should not be attempted by pianists;* they are for feet only! For the sake of facility, the pedal lines move stepwise and stay within an octave. Players who improvise in the jazz sense can "take off" from the melody and the chord symbols.

The chord symbols also are designed for pianists who have studied the popular chord method; players can read the melody line and improvise their own left-hand accompaniments. The chord symbols may be used, too, by bass players (string or brass); just play the root note of each symbol, except where another note is indicated (for example, "D/F# bass"). Accordionists can use the chord symbols for the left-hand buttons while playing the treble portions of the arrangement as written.

—*The Editors*

UNFORGETTABLE

SECTION ONE

THE NEW "STANDARD" HITS OF THE '50s

The beguiling lilt and quiet warmth of this song made it a perfect fit for the mellow, honey-and-sand voice of Nat "King" Cole. It was a No. 1 hit for the unforgettable Nat in 1951. Forty years later, daughter Natalie Cole recorded a "duet" with her father, and "Unforgettable" hit the charts once again.

In a relaxed 4 (♪♪ played as ♪³♪)

Words and Music by Irving Gordon

Un-for-get-ta-ble, _____ that's what you are; _____
un-for-get-ta-ble, _____ in ev-'ry way; _____

Un-for-get-ta-ble, _____ though near or
And for-ev-er-more, _____ that's how you'll

far. _____
stay. _____

Like a song of
That's why, dar - ling,

love that clings_ to me,
it's in - cred - i - ble

how the thought of
that some - one so

you does things_ to me;
un - for - get - ta - ble

1. Nev - er be - fore has some - one been more

2. thinks that I am un - for - get - ta - ble, too.

5

A Blossom Fell

England's Tin Pan Alley was tiny Denmark Street, just off Charing Cross Road in London's teeming Soho section, where the big British music publishers had their head offices. Among scores of Denmark Street hits exported to North America over the years: "These Foolish Things," "A Nightingale Sang in Berkeley Square," "If," "Goodnight Sweetheart"—and this 1955 favorite, popularized around the world by Nat "King" Cole.

Words and Music by Howard Barnes, Harold Cornelius and Dominic John

Lyrics:
A blos-som fell from off a tree, it set-tled soft-ly on the lips you turned to me. The gyp-sies say, and I know why, a fall-ing blos-som on-ly touch-es lips that lie. A blos-som

7

Moments to Remember

If any one song evokes the pre-Elvis '50s, it's this anthem to high-school good times. Senior proms, football games, white bucks and drive-in movies were still creating vivid memories when The Four Lads sang this 1955 hit. It may not have been the year's best-seller ("Davy Crockett" and "The Yellow Rose of Texas" took care of that), but what could top a song that reduced even the most muscle-bound of football heroes to blubbering incoherence on graduation day?

Words by Al Stillman; Music by Robert Allen

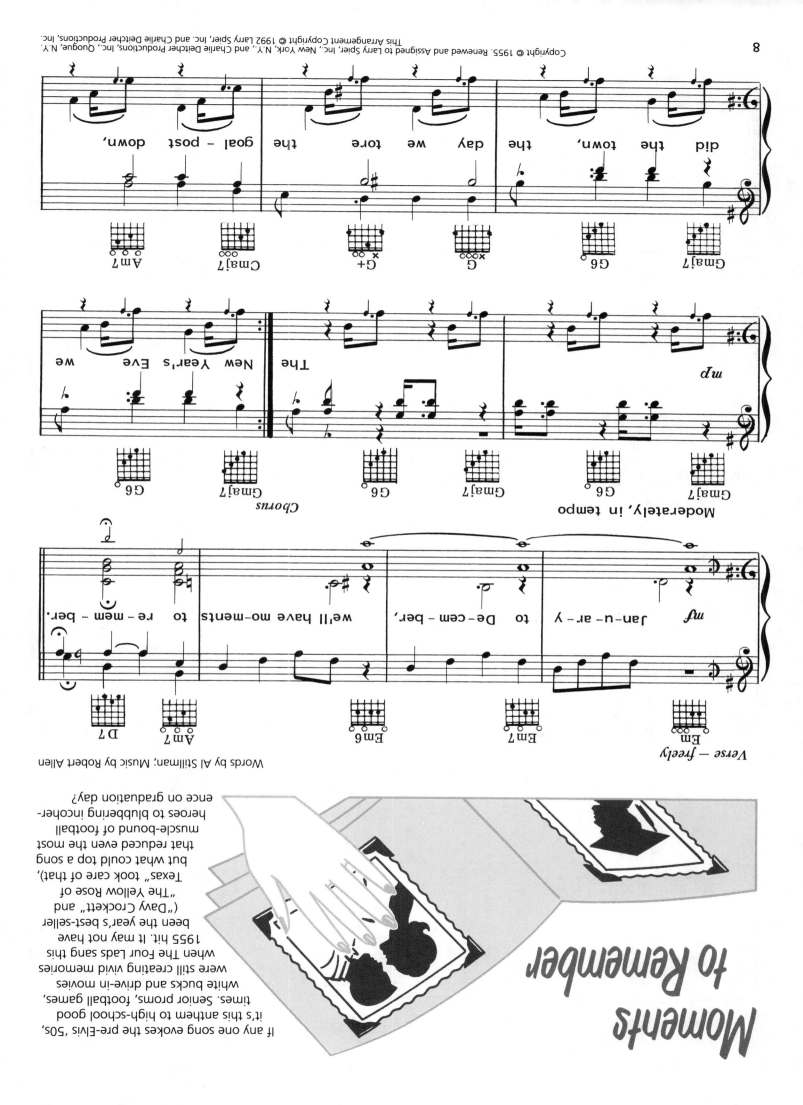

we will have these mo-ments to re-mem - ber. The

qui - et walks, the nois - y fun, the ball-room prize we al-most won,

we will have these mo-ments to re-mem - ber. Tho'

sum-mer turns to win - ter and the pres-ent dis-ap- pears, the

Tell Me Why

Vocal groups became a national mania after The Four Aces, boyhood pals who got their start in the Philadelphia area, hit the big time in 1951 with their recording of this lover's plea. Former band pianist Al Alberts, leader and soloist of the Aces, wrote the lyrics of the song. Marty Gold, veteran arranger for another group, The Three Suns, supplied the melody.

Moderate shuffle beat

Words by Al Alberts; Music by Marty Gold

Tell me why, though I try to for-get,__ tell me why, why I think of you yet.__ I know I'll nev-er be free; What has hap-pened to me?__ Tell me why, when we danced un-til three,__ tell me why, why my heart could-n't see.__

CRY

Remember Johnnie Ray, sobbing and grimacing and tearing at his hair while intoning "If your suh-weetheart sends a letter of goodbye . . . "? Parents hated him—but tearful teens sobbed right along as "Cry" shot to No.1 on *Your Hit Parade* in 1952 and stayed there for five weeks. The flip side of "Cry," the equally weepy "Little White Cloud That Cried," went to No. 2.

Words and Music by Churchill Kohlman

* Chord symbols represent a simplified version of the piano part.

The Naughty Lady of Shady Lane

As Roy Bennett recalled it, whenever his wife or Sid Tepper's wife was pregnant, the songwriting team ("Red Roses for a Blue Lady") had a hit. Mrs. Tepper was expecting in 1955 when the composers' tale of a precocious *femme fatale*— recorded by The Ames Brothers—racked up 15 weeks on the charts.

Words and Music by Roy C. Bennett and Sid Tepper

Moderately

The naugh-ty la - dy of Shad-y Lane__ has the town in a whirl. The naugh-ty la - dy of Shad-y Lane,__ me oh, my oh, what a girl!

1. The naugh-ty la - dy of Shad-y Lane__ has hit the town__ like a

2.

You should see__ how she car - ries on__ with her ad-mir - ers ga-

3. The things they're try - ing to pin on her__ won't hold much wa - ter I'm

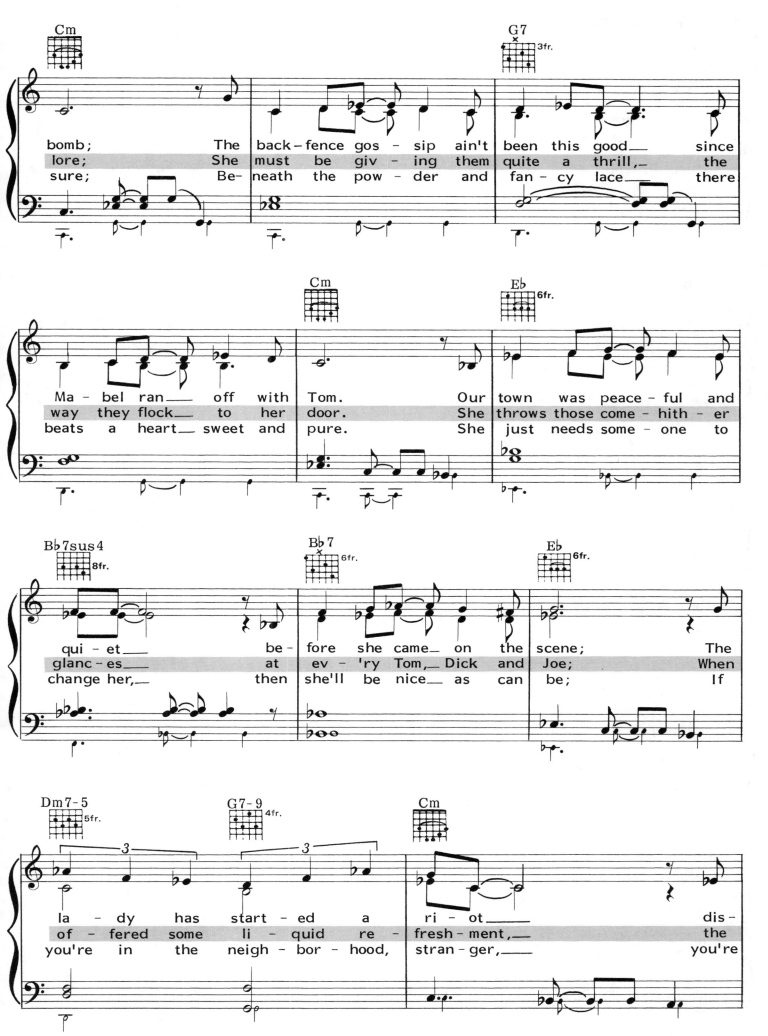

8va lower (piano only)- - - - - -

The Hawaiian Wedding Song

Charles E. King, Hawaiian politician and composer (he also penned "Song of the Islands"), wrote the melody and original lyrics of this song in 1926. He called it "Waiting for Thee," and it had no more to do with weddings than the melody that became the "Anniversary Song" originally had to do with anniversaries—but it was heard so often at the altar that people made the connection anyway. Al Hoffman and Dick Manning added a new title and lyrics in 1958, Andy Williams recorded the result and—*voilà!*—a hit was born.

English Words by Al Hoffman and Dick Manning; Hawaiian Words and Music by Charles E. King

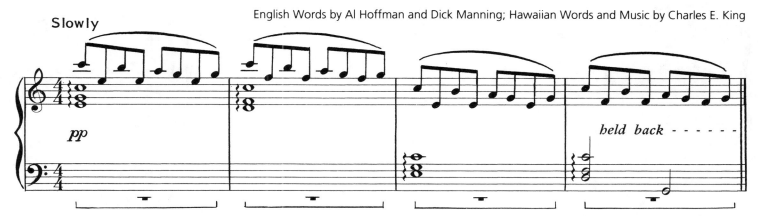

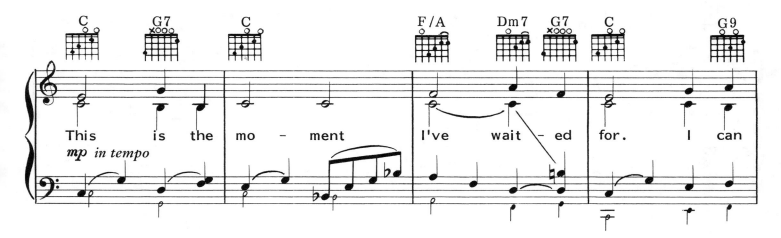

This is the mo - ment I've wait - ed for. I can

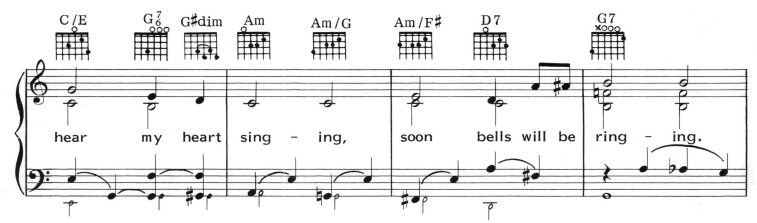

hear my heart sing - ing, soon bells will be ring - ing.

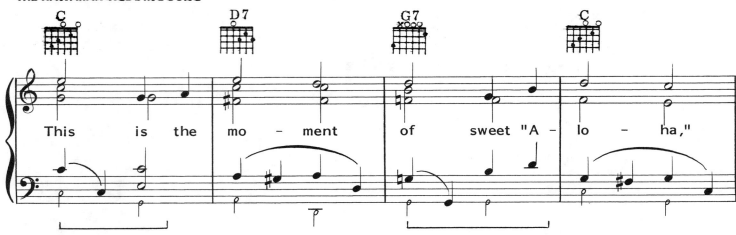

This is the mo - ment of sweet "A - lo - ha,"

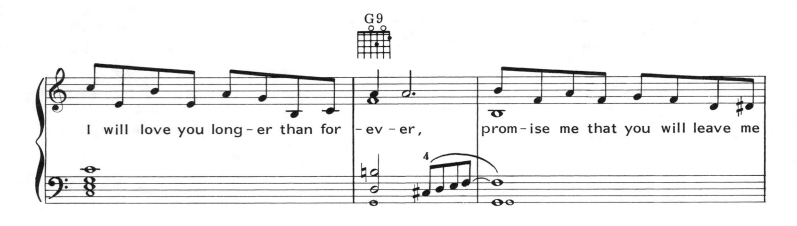

I will love you long - er than for - ev - er, prom - ise me that you will leave me

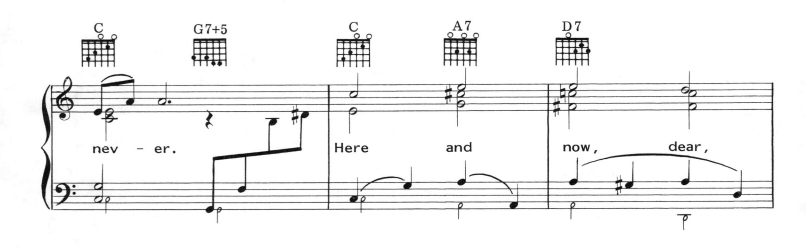

nev - er. Here and now, dear,

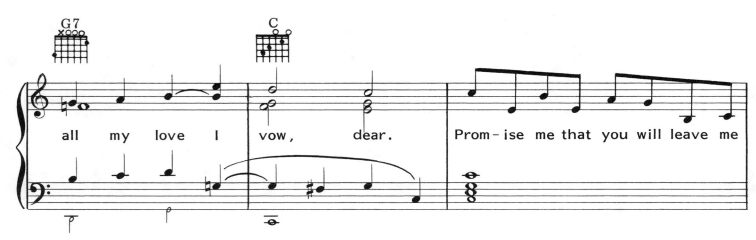

all my love I vow, dear. Prom - ise me that you will leave me

Catch a Falling Star

Is it possible these days to imagine a top TV show featuring a relaxed guy in a V-neck cardigan, perched on a stool singing? Well, that was precisely the formula of the very popular *Perry Como Show*. And during that hit show's long run and Perry's even longer career, the laid-back crooner produced dozens of hit records of songs like this 1958 gem. Other No. 1 Como tunes of the '50s include "Don't Let the Stars Get in Your Eyes," "Hot Diggity" and "Round and Round."

Words and Music by Paul J. Vance and Lee Pockriss

22

Misty

Imagine it's 1954. A group of musicians are in a recording studio: Fats Heard on drums, Bull Ruther on bass and, at the piano, the unique Erroll Garner, picking out a tune. "Hey, man," says Heard, "play that again . . . " It was a melody Garner had been fooling with, opening on a three-note drop to the major seventh. A bit of sweat, a lot of genius and a big contribution from lyricist Johnny Burke, and those three little notes grew into "Misty." A hit record by Johnny Mathis in 1959, and another great standard was off and running.

Words by Johnny Burke; Music by Erroll Garner

MISTY

you._____ On my own, would I wan-der through this won-der-land a - lone, nev-er know-ing my right foot from my left, my hat_____ from my glove?_____ I'm too mist-y and too much in love._____

Enjoy Yourself
(It's Later Than You Think)

Here's a song with a message for any era and all generations: Go out and have a ball. Tommy Dorsey, with supreme bad judgment, recorded the tune in 1948 without a vocal. Nothing happened. Guy Lombardo and his saxophonist-songwriter brother, Carmen, spotted it soon after. "The lyrics are the message," said Carmen. The Lombardo band's recording of "Enjoy Yourself" scored a major success in 1950.

Words and Music by Herb Magidson and Carl Sigman

Brightly, like a samba

You work and work for years and years, you're al-ways on the go; You've
gon-na take that o-cean trip no mat-ter come what may; You've

nev-er take a min-ute off, too bus-y mak-ing dough. Some-
got your res-er-va-tions, but you just can't get a-way. Next

Chorus

day, you say, you'll have your fun when you're a mil-lion-aire; Im-
year for sure you'll see the world, you'll real-ly get a-round. But

ag-ine all the fun you'll have in your old rock-in' chair.
how far can you trav-el when you're six feet un-der-ground.

En-

joy your-self, it's lat-er than you think! En-

joy your-self, while you're still in the pink. The

28

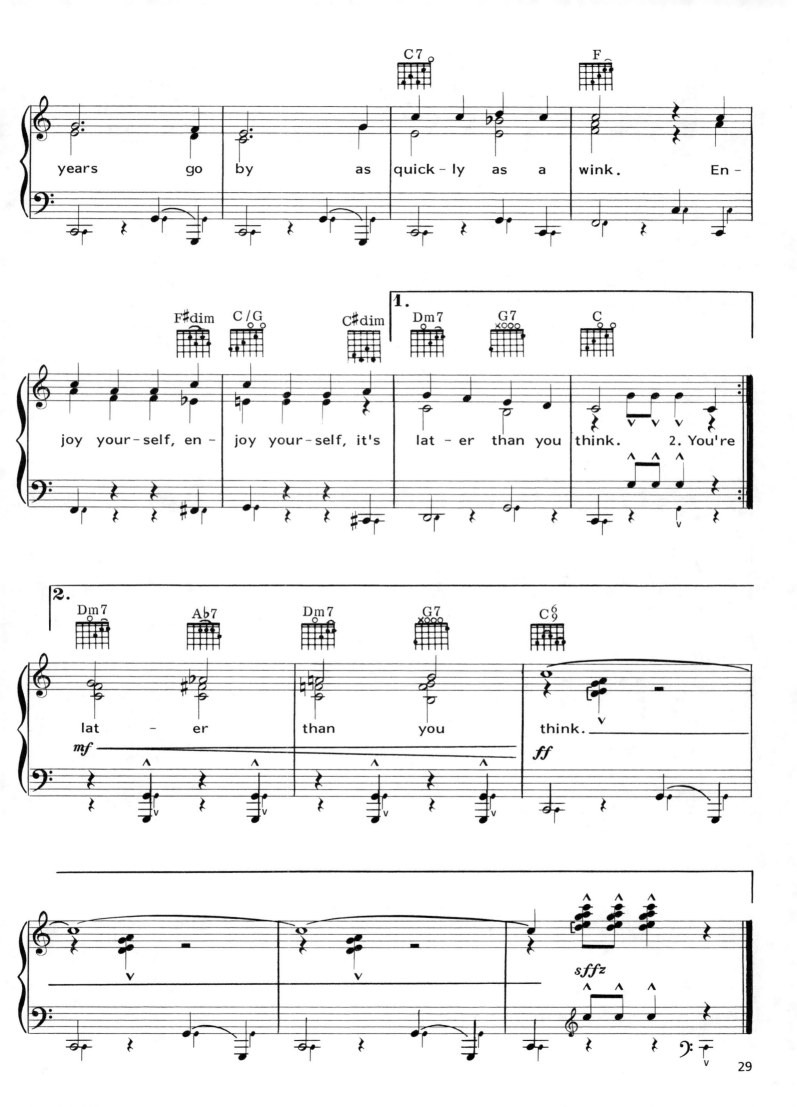

THE OLD PIANO ROLL BLUES

This old-timey honky-tonk tune isn't really so old-timey at all. New Jerseyite Cy ("Sweet Violets") Coben wrote it in 1949, and it hit the charts the next year, thanks to recordings by Hoagy Carmichael and Cass Daley and boogie-woogie pianist Lawrence Cook. One interesting side effect: the tune spurred a fad for player pianos and a glut of such nostalgic ditties as "Music! Music! Music!" and "Dearie."

Moderate ragtime tempo (♪♪ played as ♪³♪)

Words and Music by Cy Coben

I wan-na hear it a-gain,— I wan-na hear it a-gain,—

The Old Pi-an-o Roll Blues.— We're sit-tin' at an up-right, my

sweet-ie and me,— push-in' on the ped-als mak-in' sweet har-mo-ny. When we hear

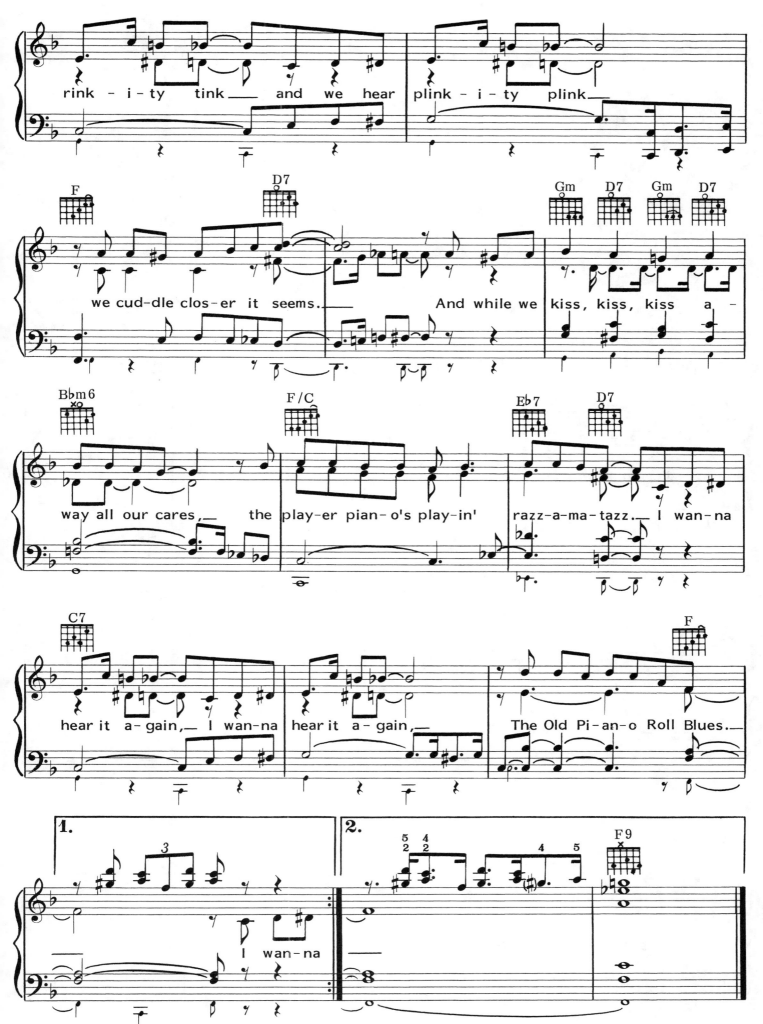

I'm Walking Behind You

The success of this 1953 English import by Billy Reid, who also composed "The Gypsy" and "A Tree in the Meadow," celebrated the return of pop music idol Eddie Fisher after two years of service in the Army. While he was away, two Fisher discs came out: "Lady of Spain" and "Wish You Were Here." Both had been recorded before he donned a uniform and were held for release during his absence.

Words and Music by Billy Reid

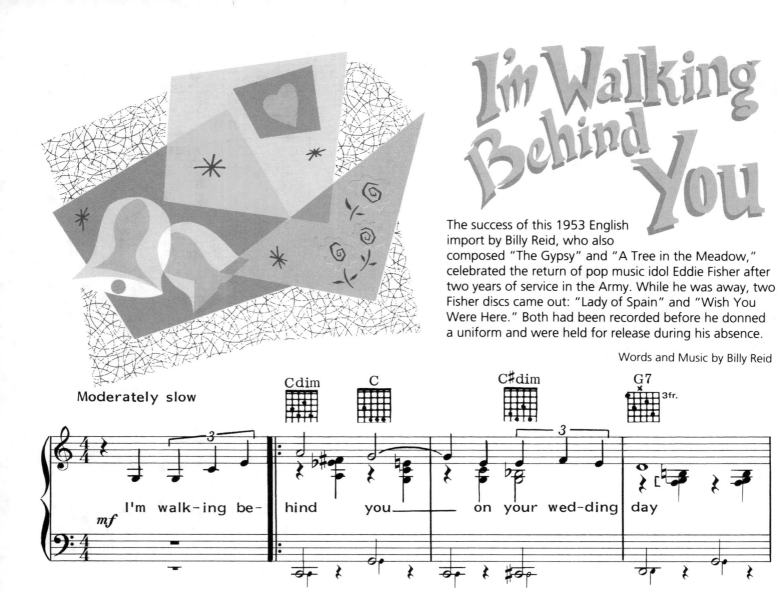

Moderately slow

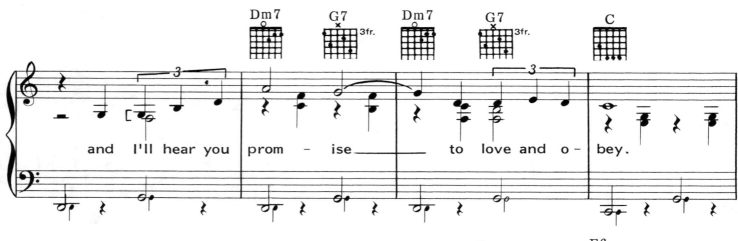

I'm walk-ing be- hind you on your wed-ding day and I'll hear you prom - ise to love and o- bey.

Though you may for- get me, you're still on my mind;

French popular songs, sometimes passionate to a point verging on melodrama, have often done well on this side of the Atlantic. Witness the success of "La Vie en Rose," "Beyond the Sea," "It Must Be Him" and dozens of others. This 1957 French import produced popular recordings for both Tony Bennett and pianist Roger Williams.

Words by Carl Sigman; Music by Charles Danvers

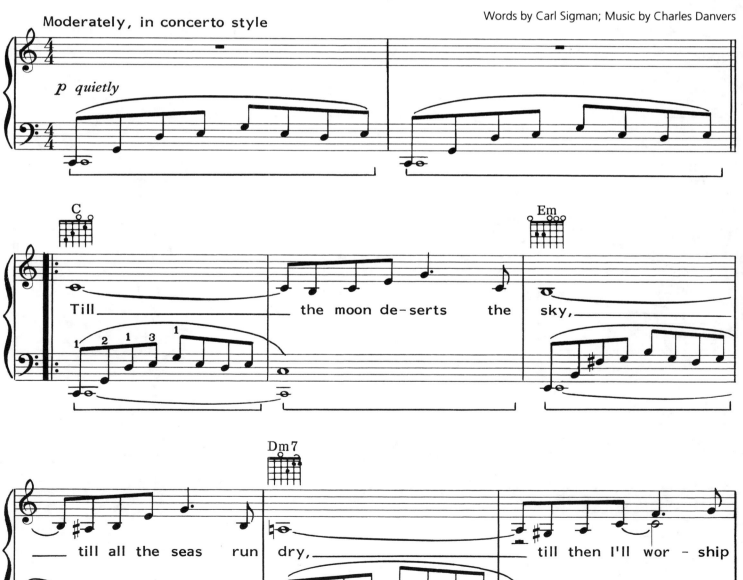

Moderately, in concerto style

p quietly

Till_____ the moon de-serts the sky,_____

_____ till all the seas run dry,_____ till then I'll wor - ship

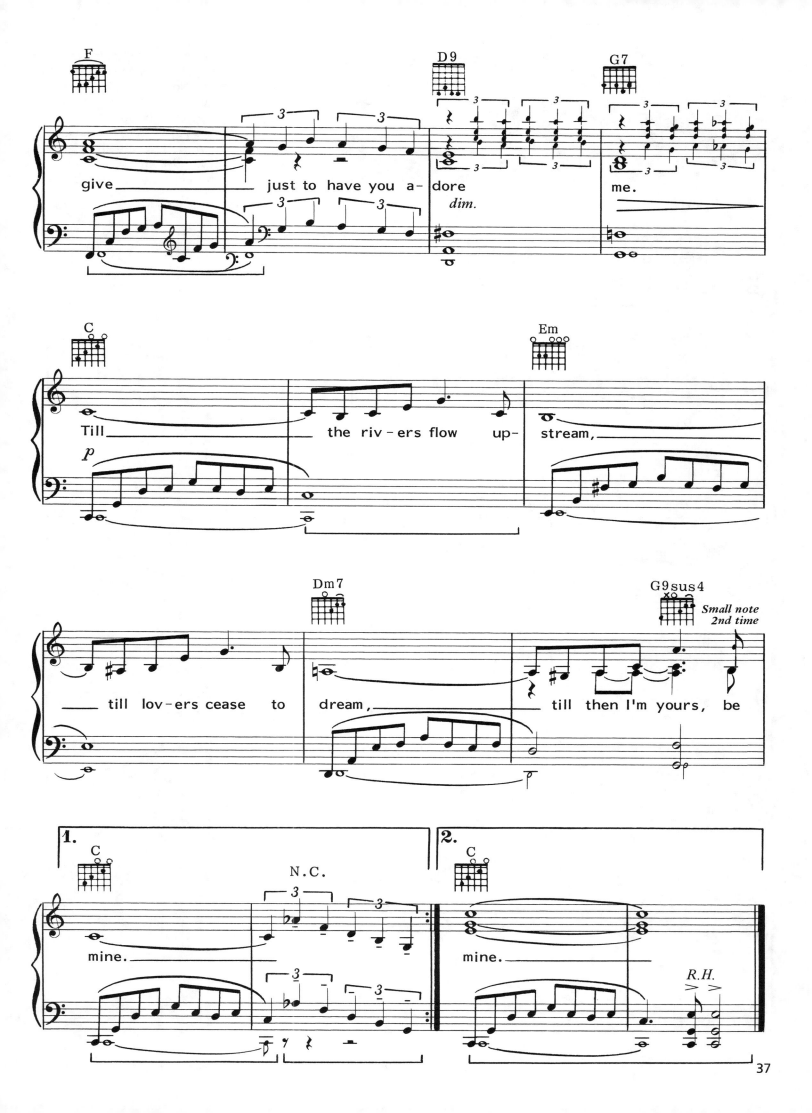

TOO YOUNG

Sylvia Dee and Sid Lippman's ode to puppy love provided Nat "King" Cole with a No. 1 hit in 1951. The song will always have a sentimental pull for those who were "too young" in the '50s. But hearing it today, the same people—now "fifty-something"— might wonder why they were in such a big hurry to grow up.

Slowly

Words by Sylvia Dee; Music by Sid Lippman

I BELIEVE

World War II wasn't long over when we found ourselves in another conflict, this time an undeclared "police action" in far-off Korea. It was a time to test faith, and when singer Jane Froman introduced what composer Ervin Drake termed "a song to give the average person hope," "I Believe" was an overnight sensation. Frankie Laine's record, an emotional declaration of faith, sold millions and caused the song to appear on *Your Hit Parade* for 23 weeks.

Words and Music by Ervin Drake, Irvin Graham, Jimmy Shirl and Al Stillman

Maestoso (Slow and stately)

I BELIEVE

Vaya con Dios
(May God Be with You)

This Spanish-flavored perennial (the title translates as "Go with God") was written in Hollywood in 1953. It was a long-running No. 1 hit for Les Paul and Mary Ford, whose multitracked guitar-voice duets pioneered the new techniques that soon transformed the recording industry.

Words and Music by Larry Russell, Inez James and Buddy Pepper

43

VAYA CON DIOS

vil-lage mis-sion bells are soft-ly ring-ing,
dawn is break-ing through a gray to-mor-row, if you but the

lis-ten with your heart you'll hear them sing-ing.
mem-o-ries we share are there to bor-row.

Va-ya con Di-os, my dar-ling;
Va-ya con Di-os, my dar-ling;

May God be with you, my love. *(continue to next page)*
May God be with you, my love. *(end here _____)*
2nd time, slower

Till I Waltz Again with You

How many of the fans who bought Teresa Brewer's No. 1 record in 1952 realized that this ode to romance in three-quarter time was not a waltz at all? All the same, the song—her second million-seller after "Music! Music! Music!"—helped put the 21-year-old Miss Brewer's career in high-flying orbit.

Words and Music by Sidney Prosen

Lilting (♫ played as ♩♪)

Till I waltz a-gain with you ____ let no oth-er hold your

charms; ____ If my dreams should all come true ____

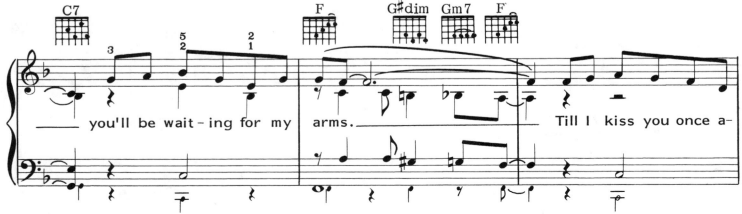

____ you'll be wait-ing for my arms. ____ Till I kiss you once a-

TILL I WALTZ AGAIN WITH YOU

so." Till I waltz a-gain with you,_____ just the way we are to-

night,_____ I will keep my prom-ise

true,_____ for you are my guid-ing

light, my light, my light. I will keep my prom-ise true,_____

for you are my guid-ing light.

What a Diff'rence a Day Made

(Cuando Vuelva a Tu Lado)

The original title of this Mexican import translates as "When I Return to Your Side." Stanley Adams ("There Are Such Things") contributed an English lyric and a new title in 1934, and "What a Diff'rence a Day Made" has been a favorite of singers and instrumentalists ever since. Dinah Washington, until then known chiefly in the rhythm-and-blues field, won a Grammy with her 1959 recording of it, belatedly becoming a "mainstream" pop and soul star.

English Words by Stanley Adams; Music and Spanish Words by Maria Grever

Moderately slow beguine

No Chord

What a dif-f'rence a day made! Twen-ty-four lit-tle
Cuan-do vuel-va a tu la-do, no me nie-gues tus

hours brought the sun and the flow-ers
be-sos, que el a-mor que te he da-do,

where there used to be rain. My yes-ter-day was
no po-drás ol-vi-dar. No me pre-gun-tes

Who's Sorry Now?

This oldie was a tearjerker for vaudevillians Van and Schenck until jazz bands hiked up the tempo in the late '20s. It remained a Dixieland specialty until 1957, when Connie Francis put it to a slow rock beat and converted it back into a weepie. Her record stayed on the charts for 22 weeks and made her a star.

Words by Bert Kalmar and Harry Ruby; Music by Ted Snyder

Right to the end, just like a friend, I tried to warn you some-how. You had your way, now you must pay; I'm glad that you're sor - ry now.

1. now.

2. now.

Melody of Love

Written in 1903, this beloved old waltz has had several bursts of popularity. Wayne King made it a radio hit in 1942 as background music to Franklyn MacCormack's recitation of a poem called "Why Do I Love You?" It scored again in the '50s in a vocal version by The Four Aces with lyrics by folksinger Tom Glazer, and yet again as an instrumental recording by Billy Vaughn.

Words by Tom Glazer; Music by Hans Engelmann

MY PRAYER

"Avant de Mourir" ("Before Dying") is the rather morbid original title of this evergreen, written as a violin solo in 1926 by French fiddler Georges Boulanger. As "My Prayer," with a lyric by Jimmy ("Harbor Lights," "Red Sails in the Sunset") Kennedy, it was a hit for Glenn Miller in 1939 and, of course, for The Platters, in 1956.

Words and musical adaptation by Jimmy Kennedy; Music by Georges Boulanger

BLUEBERRY HILL

Lots of performers have done well with this hardy perennial, written for a Gene Autry film in 1940. It was big for Glenn Miller and His Orchestra, and was also recorded by Louis Armstrong. But for fans of the '50s those opening words, "I found my thrill . . . ," could only be intoned by the inimitable Antoine "Fats" Domino.

Medium rock and roll tempo

Words and Music by Al Lewis, Larry Stock and Vincent Rose

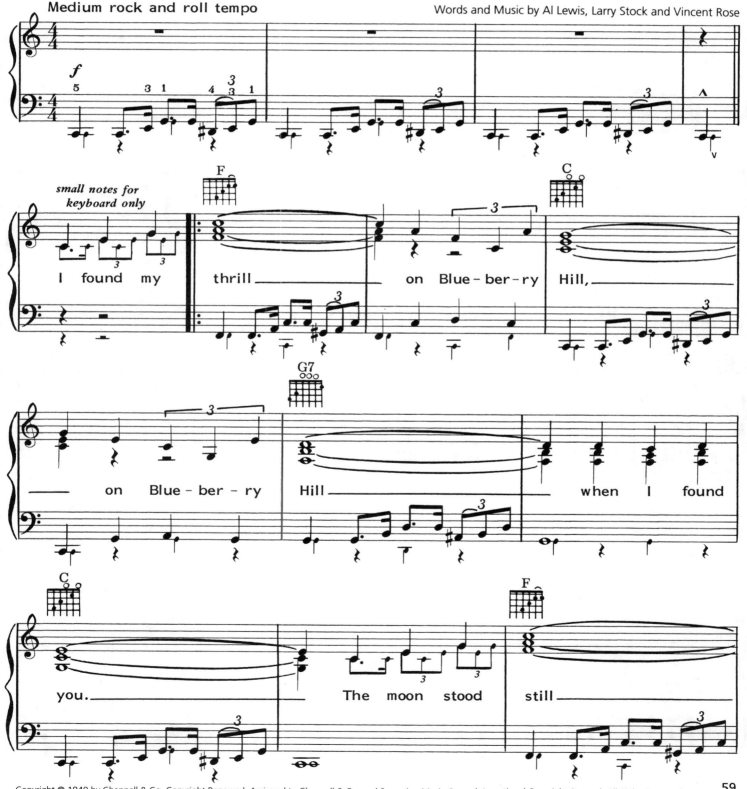

small notes for keyboard only

I found my thrill ____ on Blue - ber - ry Hill, ____ on Blue - ber - ry Hill ____ when I found you. ____ The moon stood still ____

LOVE LETTERS IN THE SAND

Newspaperman and sometime pop poet Nick Kenny published these verses in his New York *Daily Mirror* column one day in 1931. (Brother Charles helped out on the poem.) Songwriter J. Fred ("You Go to My Head") Coots liked it and wrote a melody for it. Russ Columbo and bandleader George Hall made "Love Letters in the Sand" a standard in the '30s, and Pat Boone had a major hit with it in 1957.

Words by Nick and Charles Kenny; Music by J. Fred Coots

It Isn't Fair

Bandleader Richard Himber won friends for this composition in the
'30s by using it as the theme song for his regular *Studebaker Hour*
broadcasts from New York's Essex House Hotel. Sammy Kaye revived
"It Isn't Fair" at the start of the '50s with a record featuring a vocal by
Don Cornell. It brought the big-voiced singer to wide public attention, and
helped launch his successful solo career.

Words by Richard Himber; Music by Frank Warshauer and Sylvester Sprigato

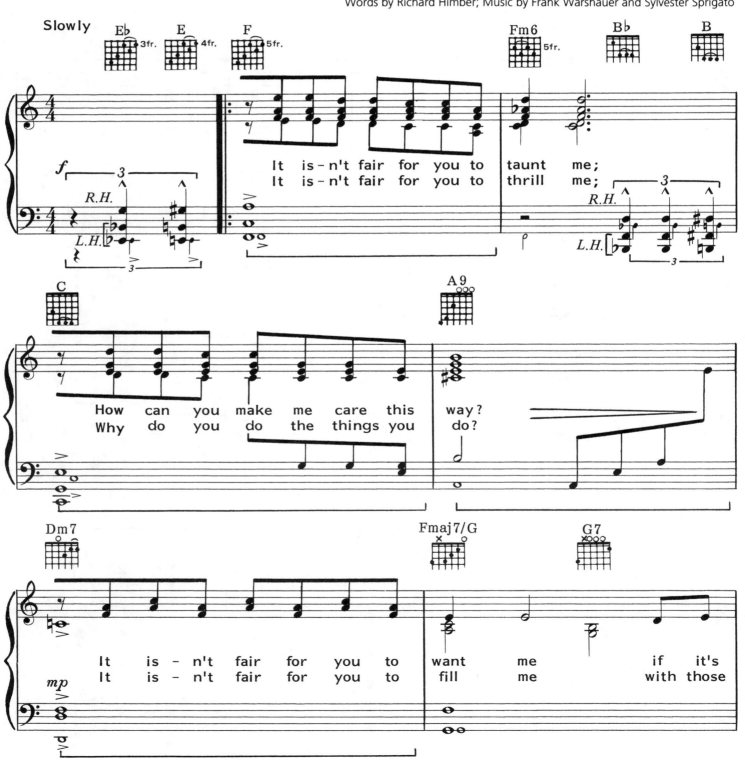

It is-n't fair for you to taunt me;
It is-n't fair for you to thrill me;

How can you make me care this way?
Why do you do the things you do?

It is-n't fair for you to want me if it's
It is-n't fair for you to fill me with those

I Apologize

Billy Eckstine—"Mr. B." to his fans—revived this 1931 confection in 1951. Russian-born co-composer Al Hoffman's three decades of hits include "Heartaches," "Mairzy Doats," "Takes Two to Tango," "Papa Loves Mambo" and "If I Knew You Were Comin' (I'd've Baked a Cake)."

Words and Music by Al Hoffman, Al Goodhart and Ed Nelson

P.S. I Love You

Johnny Mercer wasn't just a songwriter—he was an original, a folk poet able to tap the basic emotions of all listeners. This 1934 gem, revived by The Hilltoppers in 1953, is just one of many Mercer lyrics that have touched us all. Other Mercerian odes include "How Little We Know," "That Old Black Magic," "Moon River," "In the Cool, Cool, Cool of the Evening" and "Autumn Leaves."

Words by Johnny Mercer; Music by Gordon Jenkins

Fascination

This old favorite began life in Europe in 1904 as a *valse tzigane,* a waltz in gypsy style. It won new fans in 1957 as the sound-track theme for the Audrey Hepburn–Gary Cooper movie *Love in the Afternoon* and as a chart-topping record by *chanteuse* Jane Morgan, fresh home from a singing career in France.

Music by F.D. Marchetti; English Words by Dick Manning

Slow waltz

p very gracefully

It was fas-ci- na - tion, I know,_____ and it might have end-ed right then at the start._____ Just a pass-ing glance,_____ just a brief ro- mance,_____ and I might have gone on my way emp-ty-heart - ed._____ It was fas-ci-

73

It's All in the Game

Charles Gates Dawes was best known as Calvin Coolidge's vice-president in the '20s and co-winner of the 1925 Nobel Peace Prize. Earlier, in 1912, while working as a banker in Chicago, he wrote the melody that, with a lyric by Carl Sigman, became this favorite, a hit twice in the '50s for singer Tommy Edwards (in 1951 and again in 1958).

Words by Carl Sigman; Music by Charles Gates Dawes

SECTION THREE

HIT SONGS FROM HIT SHOWS

BAUBLES, BANGLES AND BEADS

Like the rest of the music from Robert Wright and George Forrest's 1953 Broadway hit *Kismet,* "Baubles, Bangles and Beads" is drawn from the works of Alexander Borodin (1833-87). (The lovely melody is an only slightly altered version of the scherzo from the Russian composer's String Quartet No. 2 in D.) The song became a hit for veteran jazz trumpeter Jonah Jones, who recorded it over a shuffle rhythm in 1957 and came up with a successor to his earlier best-seller from Broadway, "On the Street Where You Live."

from *Kismet*
Words and Music by Robert Wright and George Forrest; based on a theme by Alexander Borodin

Graceful waltz

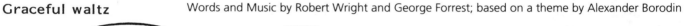

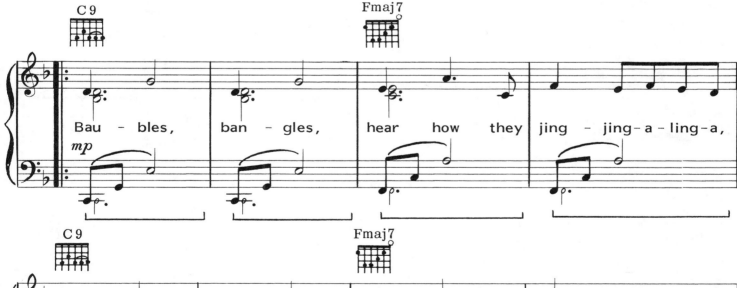

Bau - bles, ban - gles, hear how they jing - jing-a-ling-a, bau - bles, ban - gles, bright shin - y beads.

BAUBLES, BANGLES AND BEADS

Stranger in Paradise

The musical Arabian Night that is *Kismet* takes place in long-ago Baghdad over the course of a day. This beauty from the show is one of the "Polovetsian Dances" found in Alexander Borodin's opera *Prince Igor*. It provided a best-selling recording for the young Tony Bennett in 1953.

Moderately from *Kismet* Words and Music by Robert Wright and George Forrest; based on a theme by Alexander Borodin

Take my hand, I'm a stran-ger in par-a-dise, all lost in a won-der-land, a stran-ger in par-a-dise. If I stand star-ry-eyed, that's a dan-ger in par-a-dise for mor-tals who

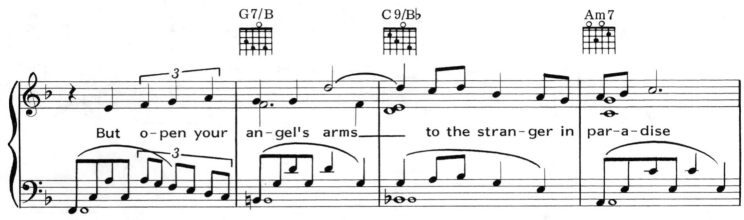

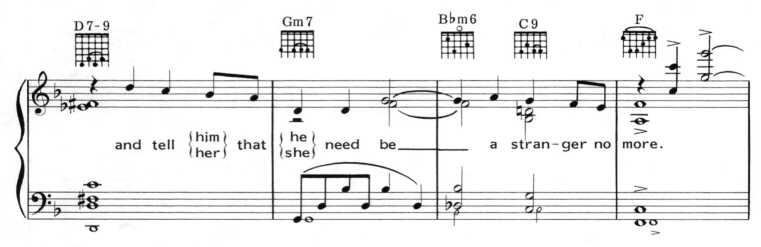

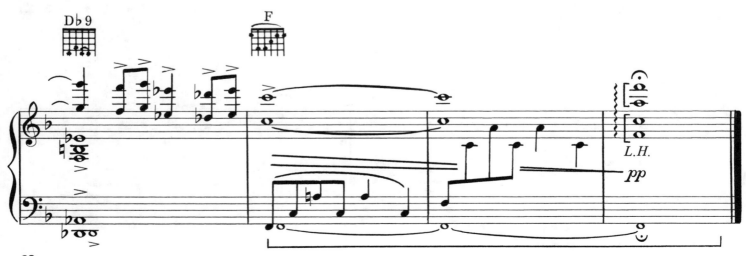

Hello, Young Lovers

The 19th-century novel *Anna and the King of Siam,* based on Anna Leonowens' diaries, *The English Governess at the Siamese Court,* was in turn the basis for Rodgers and Hammerstein's 1951 Broadway hit *The King and I.* In this song, the English schoolmistress tries to tell the ladies of the King's court of the happiness she shared with her late husband.

from *The King and I*   Words by Oscar Hammerstein II; Music by Richard Rodgers

Graceful waltz

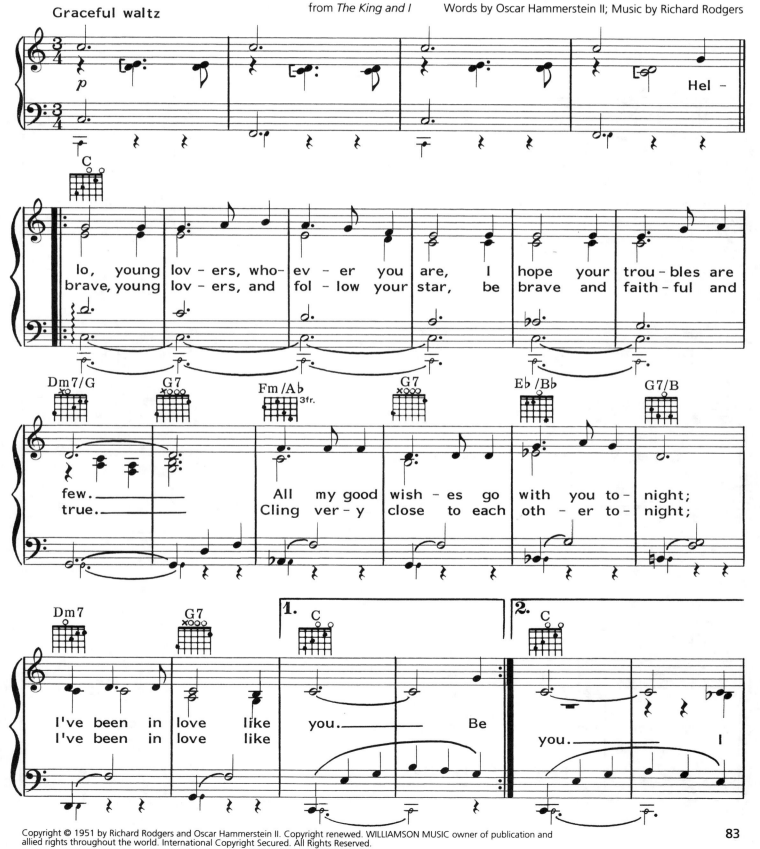

Hel-lo, young lov-ers, who-ev-er you are, I hope your trou-bles are few.
brave, young lov-ers, and fol-low your star, be brave and faith-ful and true.

All my good wish-es go with you to-night;
Cling ver-y close to each oth-er to-night;

I've been in love like you.
I've been in love like

1. you. Be

2. you. I

HELLO, YOUNG LOVERS

I Whistle a Happy Tune

The King and I was a Broadway smash, running for three years and even surviving the sudden and tragic death of its star, Gertrude Lawrence. One of the many memorable songs from the show is this bit of stiff-upper-lip bravado, sung by Anna to her young son when agents of the King of Siam board the ship on which she has just arrived from England.

Moderately, in 2 (♩ = 1 beat)   from *The King and I*   Words by Oscar Hammerstein II; Music by Richard Rodgers

When- ev-er I feel a-fraid, I hold my head e-rect and whis-tle a hap-py tune, so no one will sus-pect I'm a-fraid._____ While shiv-er-ing in my shoes, I strike a care-less pose and whis-tle a hap-py

Optional: Play both hands an 8va higher till the end.

"What's wrong with sweetness and light? They've been around quite awhile." The question was asked by Richard Rodgers and the philosophy it reflects applies perfectly to this title song from his final collaboration with Oscar Hammerstein II. Since its 1959 debut, *The Sound of Music* has been the most durable—and most popular—of their shows. In Hammerstein's words, "Sentiment has never been unpopular."

The Sound of Music

from *The Sound of Music*

Words by Oscar Hammerstein II; Music by Richard Rodgers

The hills are a-live with the sound of mu - sic, with songs they have sung for a thou-sand years. The hills fill my heart with the sound of mu - sic. My

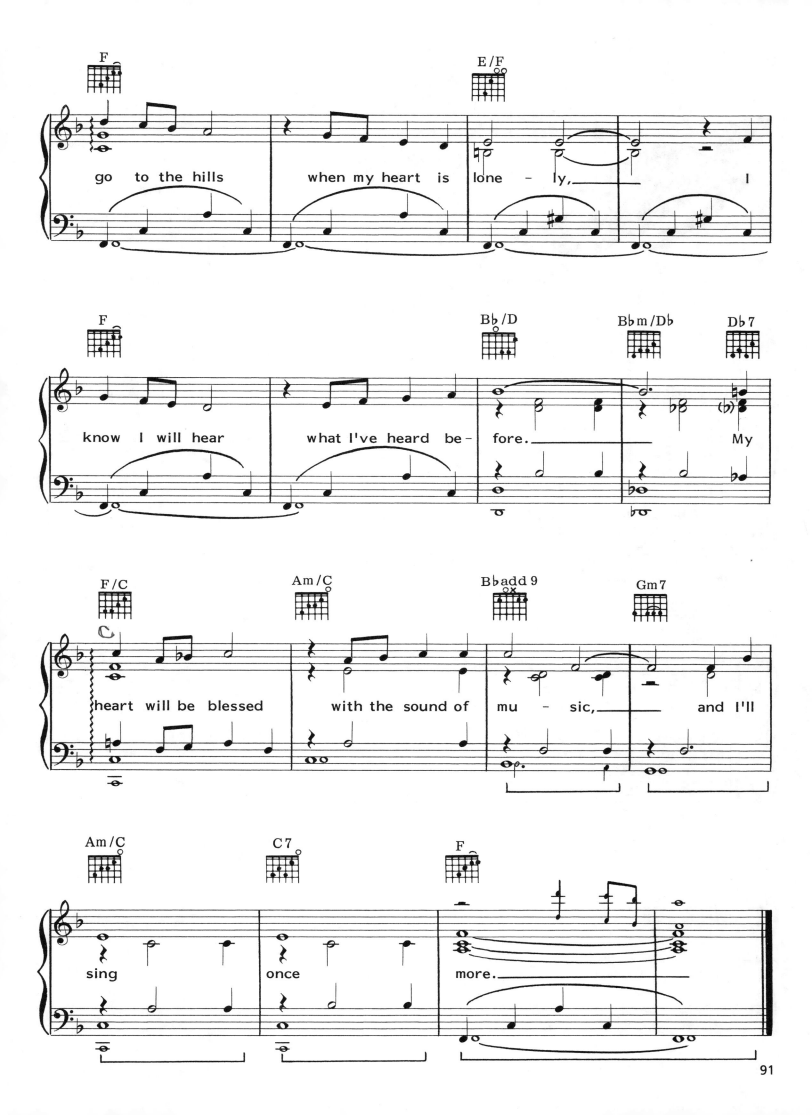

go to the hills when my heart is lone - ly,_____ I
know I will hear what I've heard be - fore._____ My
heart will be blessed with the sound of mu - sic,_____ and I'll
sing once more._____

Mack the Knife

In a sense, the vast popularity of this song in the 1950s was based on a misunderstanding. Originally titled *Moritat* ("Deed of Murder"), it described, in cold and sardonic language, a series of brutal killings attributed to the villain MacHeath, a character borrowed for *The Threepenny Opera* from John Gay's 18th-century play *The Beggar's Opera*. Marc Blitzstein's translation lightened Bertolt Brecht's words considerably, and records by Louis Armstrong, Bobby Darin and Ella Fitzgerald helped make the song a hit.

from *The Threepenny Opera*   German Words by Bertolt Brecht; English Words by Marc Blitzstein; Music by Kurt Weill

With a beat

mf

Keep the bass line smooth and even

1. Oh, the

Organ

Organ pedal doubles piano left hand except where indicated

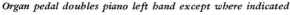

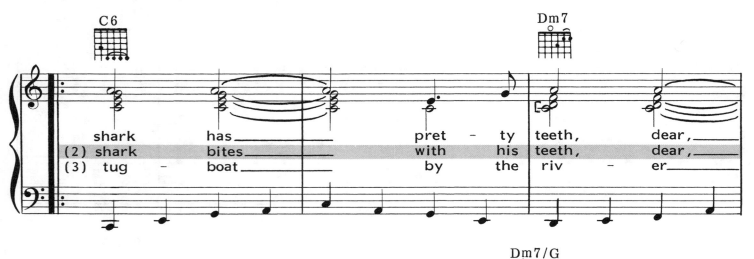

shark	has	pret - ty	teeth,	dear,
(2) shark	bites	with his	teeth,	dear,
(3) tug - boat		by the	riv -	er

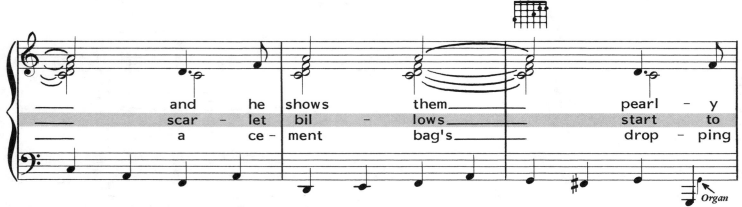

and he	shows	them	pearl -	y
scar - let	bil -	lows	start	to
a	ce - ment	bag's	drop -	ping

Organ

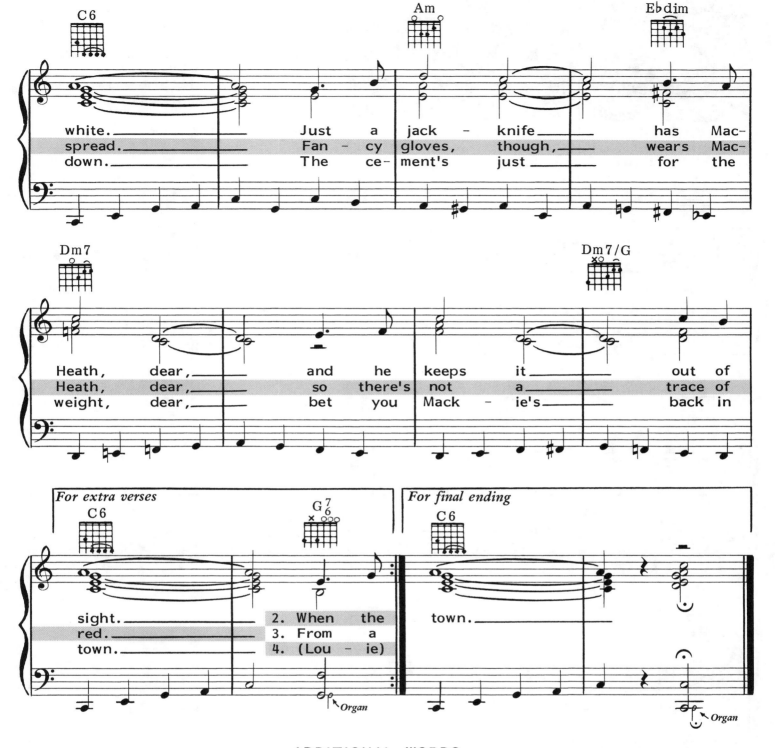

ADDITIONAL WORDS

4. (Louie) Miller disappeared, dear,
   After drawing out his cash.
   And MacHeath spends like a sailor.
   Did our boy do something rash?

5. On the sidewalk Sunday morning
   Lies a body oozing life.
   Someone's sneaking round the corner.
   Is the someone Mack the Knife?

6. Sukey Tawdry, Jenny Diver,
   Polly Peachum, Lucy Brown.
   Oh, the line forms on the right, dear,
   Now that Mackie's back in town.

Just in Time

Judy Holliday kept insisting she couldn't sing—but Jule Styne and her old friends Betty Comden and Adolph Green wrote the 1956 musical *Bells Are Ringing* as a vehicle for her anyway. The show was a hit, "Just in Time" a highlight—and a favorite with society dance bands ever after.

from *Bells Are Ringing*

Words by Betty Comden and Adolph Green; Music by Jule Styne

SEVENTY-SIX TROMBONES

Meredith Willson was his own one-man band—composer, librettist and lyricist—for *The Music Man,* the Broadway smash of 1957, and this strutting march was the show-stopper. In conceiving the musical, Willson drew on his own boyhood in Mason City, Iowa. "I didn't have to make anything up," he said. "All I had to do was remember."

from *The Music Man*　　　　Words and Music by Meredith Willson

Brisk march (in 2; ♩. = 1 beat)

Sev-en-ty-
six trom - bones led the big pa - rade___ with a hun-dred and
six trom - bones caught the morn-ing sun___ with a hun-dred and
ten cor - nets close at hand.___ They were fol-lowed by
ten cor - nets right be - hind.___ There were more than a
rows and rows of the fin - est vir - tu - o - sos, the
thou - sand reeds spring - ing up like weeds, there were

big,   fat   say.   There were fif - ty mount - ed   can - non in the   bat - ter - y,

thun-der-ing, thun-der-ing loud-er than be - fore;   Clar-i-nets of

ev-'ry size and trum-pet-ers who'd im-pro-vise a   full   oc-tave high-er than the

score!   Sev-en-ty-

six   trom - bones led   the   big   pa - rade   when the or - der   to
six   trom - bones hit   the   coun - ter-point   while a hun-dred and

march rang — out loud and clear. Starting off with a
ten rang cor — nets played the air. Then I mod-est-ly

big bang — bong on a Chi — nese gong by a
took my bang place as the one and on — ly bass and I

1.
big bang — bong-er at the rear. Sev-en-ty-

2.
oom — pahed up and down the square.

I've Never Been in Love Before

The world of Damon Runyon—dames and gamblers, grifters and punks—begged to be made into a musical. Frank Loesser did just that in 1950 with the incomparable *Guys and Dolls*. This delightful song frames the romance between Salvation Army worker Miss Sarah Brown (Isabel Bigley on Broadway; Jean Simmons in the film) and Broadway sport Sky Masterson (Robert Alda; Marlon Brando).

from *Guys and Dolls*　　　　　Words and Music by Frank Loesser

Lyrics:

I've nev - er been in love be - fore, now all at once it's you, it's you for - ev - er - more. I've nev - er been in love be - fore, I thought my heart was safe, I thought I knew the score. But this is

Mr.Wonderful

Mr. Wonderful was a 1956 Broadway show that starred the ebullient Sammy Davis, Jr., as a song-and-dance man who plies his trade in Union City, New Jersey. He's finally convinced to cross the river to New York City, where he becomes a nightclub star. Olga James, playing Sammy's girlfriend, sang this lovely title theme to him. Other singers picked the song up, and Teddi King, Sarah Vaughan and Peggy Lee all had hits with it. Another tune from the show that you'll remember: "Too Close for Comfort."

from *Mr. Wonderful*   Words and Music by Jerry Bock, Larry Holofcener and George David Weiss

I Could Have Danced All Night

Who, having seen *My Fair Lady,* can forget cockney flower girl Eliza Doolittle, blossoming as a lady, expressing her delight in this unforgettable song? Julie Andrews was Eliza on Broadway; Audrey Hepburn (Marni Nixon supplied her singing voice), in the film version. An interesting sidelight: Richard Rodgers and Oscar Hammerstein were the first to try to turn George Bernard Shaw's play *Pygmalion* into a musical. They gave the project up, leaving it to Alan Jay Lerner and Fritz Loewe.

from *My Fair Lady*

Words by Alan Jay Lerner; Music by Frederick Loewe

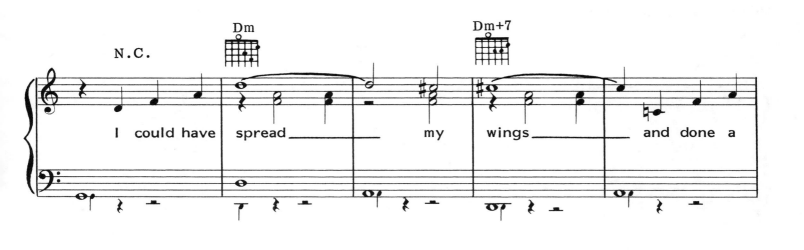

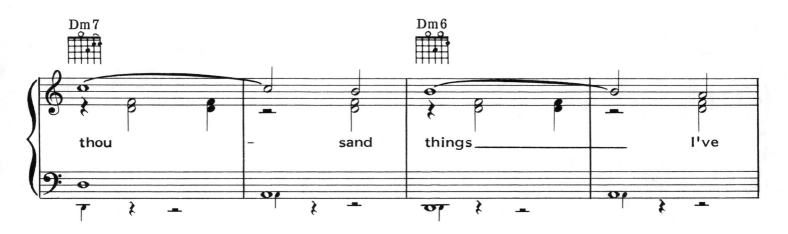

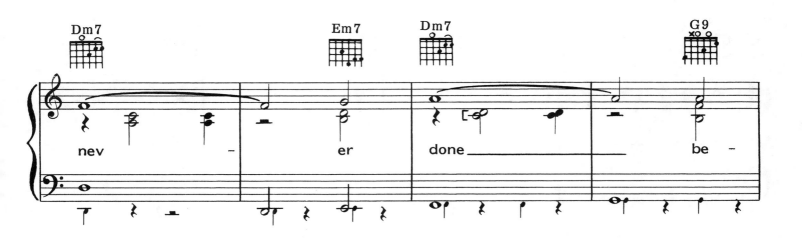

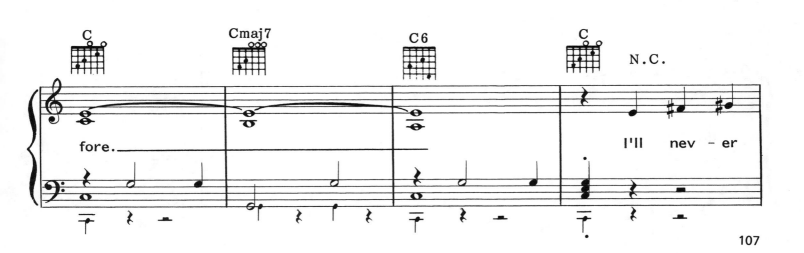

know_____ what made it so_____ ex -

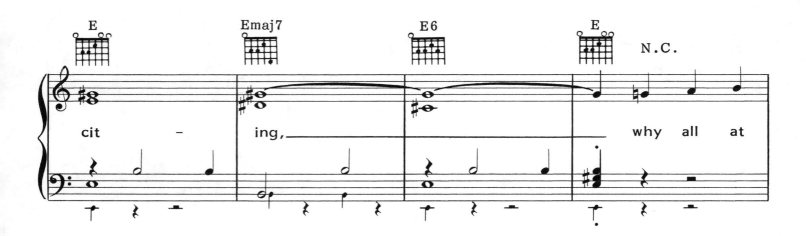

cit - ing,_____ why all at

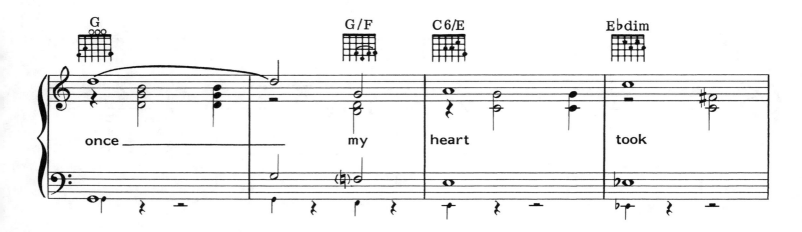

once_____ my heart took

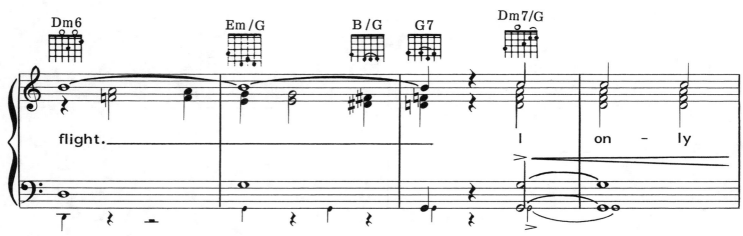

flight._____ I on - ly

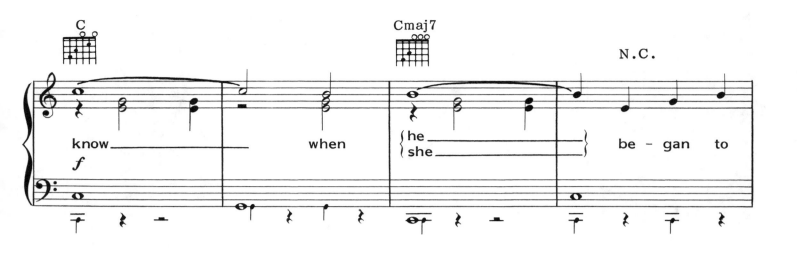

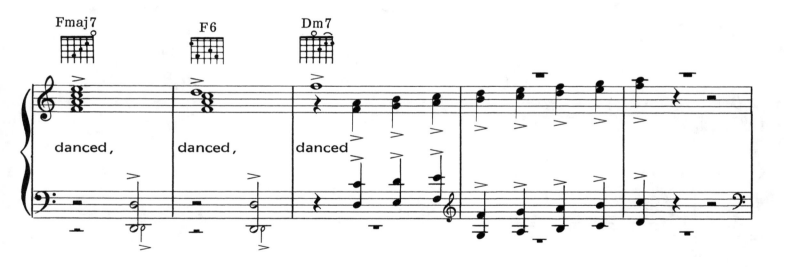

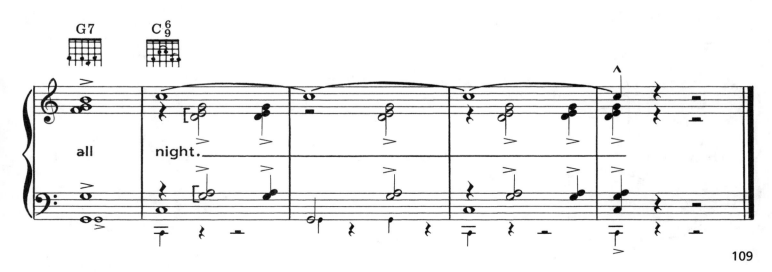

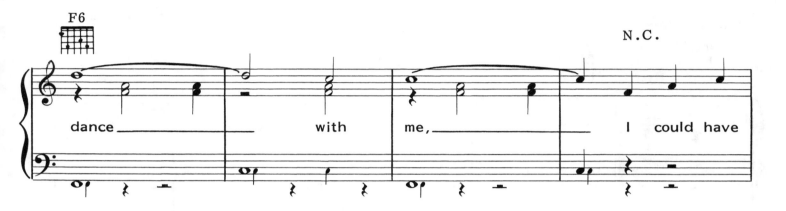

On the Street Where You Live

My Fair Lady's biggest show-stopper and only out-and-out love song began life as a non-starter. When out-of-town audiences greeted it in silence, composer Fritz Loewe demanded it be dropped. Lyricist Alan Jay Lerner disagreed. After the long middle section was replaced with an explanatory verse, "On the Street Where You Live" brought the house down every night. Balladeer Vic Damone's recording was a million-seller, followed close behind by Jonah Jones's jumping version.

from *My Fair Lady*　　　Words by Alan Jay Lerner; Music by Frederick Loewe

I have of-ten walked down this street be - fore, but the
li - lac trees in the heart of town?

pave-ment al - ways stayed be-neath my feet be - fore. All at
hear a lark in an - y oth - er part of town? Does en-

once am I sev - 'ral sto-ries high know-ing I'm on the
chant-ment pour out of ev - 'ry door? No, it's just on the

SECTION FOUR

THE BIG FILM SONGS

Love Is a Many-Splendored Thing

What did the original version of this standard sound like when Sammy Fain and Paul Francis Webster wrote it for a 1955 movie to be called *A Many-Splendored Thing*? We'll never know. Studio heads added "Love Is" to the title of the William Holden-Jennifer Jones film—and, accordingly, the veteran songwriting team came up with a brand-new, emotionally powerful song that copped that year's Oscar. Still, it's possible to wonder whether that *other* song might have been just as good.

from *Love Is a Many-Splendored Thing*   Words by Paul Francis Webster; Music by Sammy Fain

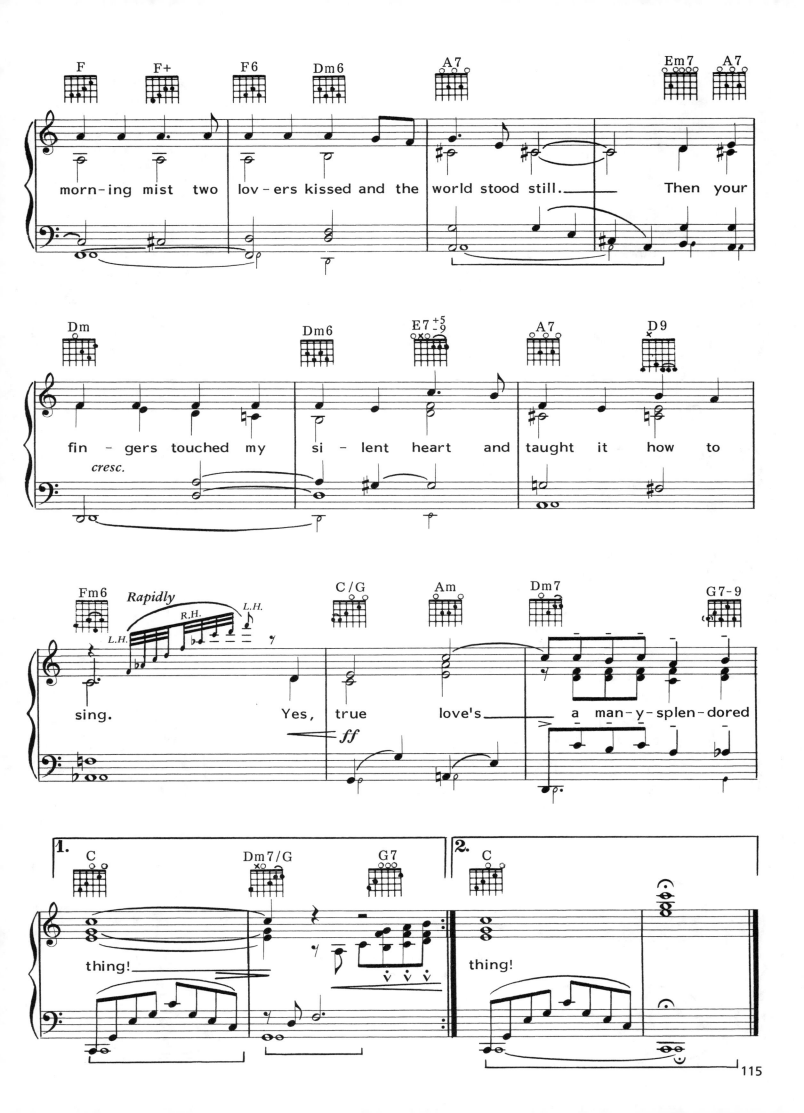

morn-ing mist two lov-ers kissed and the world stood still.___ Then your

fin - gers touched my si - lent heart and taught it how to

sing. Yes, true love's___ a man-y-splen-dored

1. thing!___ **2.** thing!

115

Strictly speaking, "Secret Love" should have been a country-and-western hit. It was part of Hollywood's 1953 sagebrush saga *Calamity Jane,* with Doris Day in the title role. Country singer Slim Whitman did, in fact, have a hit record. But Doris Day's version stayed on the pop charts for 22 weeks—four of them at the No. 1 spot—sold a million copies, and helped "Secret Love" win the Academy Award for Best Film Song.

from *Calamity Jane*   Words by Paul Francis Webster; Music by Sammy Fain

117

UNCHAINED MELODY

As is so often the case, this theme from the 1955 movie *Unchained* far outlasted the film in which it appeared. It's the work of Alex North, best known as sound-track composer for *A Streetcar Named Desire*, *Death of a Salesman*, *The Member of the Wedding* and *The Misfits*. Les Baxter's lushly scored instrumental version made the charts, as did vocal recordings (with Hy Zaret's lyrics) by both Roy Hamilton and Al Hibbler. "Unchained Melody" scored again in 1990 when The Righteous Brothers sang it on the sound track of the movie *Ghost*.

from *Unchained*   Words by Hy Zaret; Music by Alex North

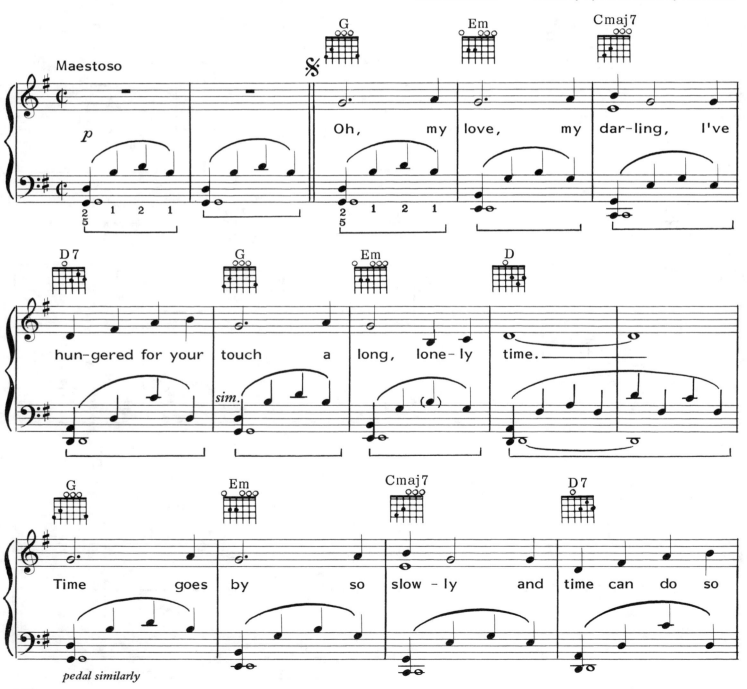

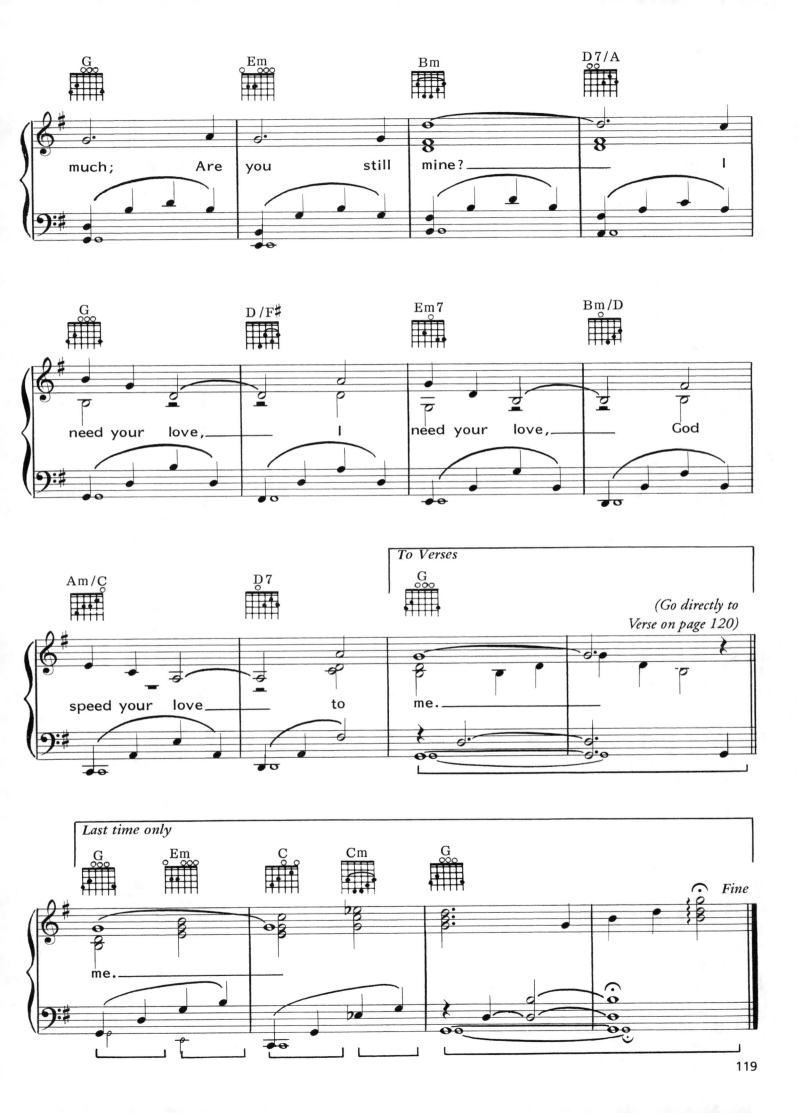

UNCHAINED MELODY

Three Coins in the Fountain

Immortalized by Italian classical composer Ottorino Respighi as one of his four *Fountains of Rome,* the ornate Fountain of Trevi carries a legend: whoever throws a coin into its waters will someday return to the Eternal City. The myth inspired both the 1954 romantic film and its Academy Award-winning title song, sung on the sound track by Frank Sinatra.

from *Three Coins in the Fountain*　　　Words by Sammy Cahn; Music by Jule Styne

Three coins in the foun-tain, each one seek-ing hap-pi-ness,

thrown by three hope-ful lov-ers. Which one will the foun-tain bless?

* Guitarists: Tune 6th string down to D.

Que Será, Será

(WHATEVER WILL BE, WILL BE)

When Alfred Hitchcock remade his 1934 suspense thriller *The Man Who Knew Too Much* in 1956, he added a few updated touches—including this song, which served as a plot device to enable a mother, played by Doris Day, to communicate with her kidnapped little boy. The lilting melody of "Que Será, Será" is so traditional sounding that it has often been mistaken for a folk song. Not only did Jay Livingston and Ray Evans's tune satisfy Hitchcock by moving the film's story ahead, it won an Academy Award in the bargain.

Simply, like a folk song

from *The Man Who Knew Too Much*   Words and Music by Jay Livingston and Ray Evans

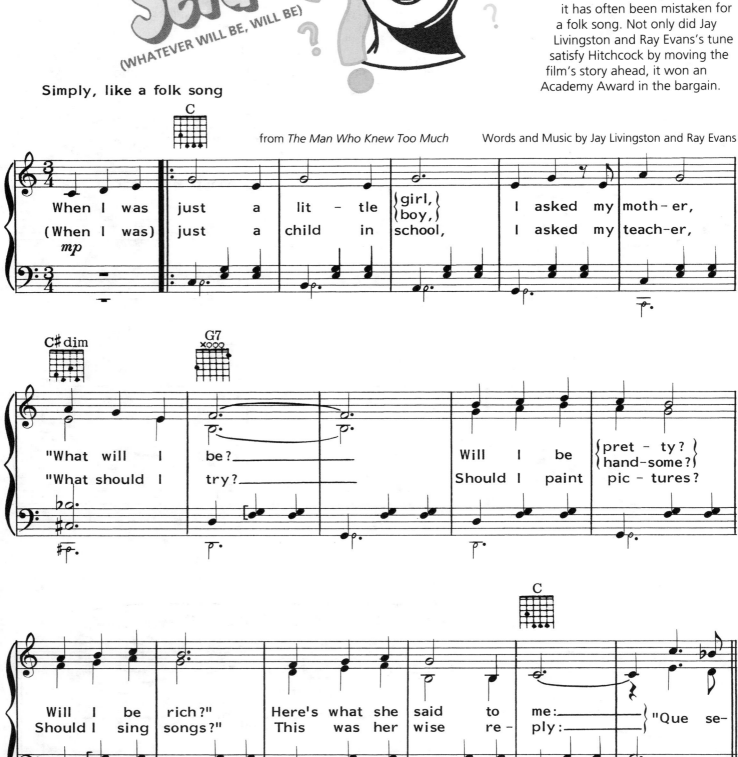

When I was just a lit - tle {girl, / boy,} I asked my moth - er,
(When I was) just a child in school, I asked my teach - er,

"What will I be?_____ Will I be {pret - ty? / hand-some?}
"What should I try?_____ Should I paint pic - tures?

Will I be rich?" Here's what she said to me:_____ {"Que se-
Should I sing songs?" This was her wise re - ply:_____

*Shake between the two notes like a marimba.

ALL THE WAY

Anyone who saw the 1957 film *The Joker Is Wild* knows the musical and dramatic importance of the big leap that the melody of this song takes to reach the line "All the way." It's the point at which Frank Sinatra, playing entertainer Joe E. Lewis, loses his voice and breaks down, unable to go on. But even without that connection "All the Way" is a deeply emotional song. It walked off with an Academy Award and has stood handsomely on its own merits ever since.

from *The Joker Is Wild*   Words by Sammy Cahn; Music by Jimmy Van Heusen

When some-bod-y loves you, it's no good un-less {he she} loves you all the way. Hap-py to be near you when you need some-one to cheer you, all the way. Tall-er than the

Gigi

Alan Jay Lerner and Frederick Loewe were riding high on the success of *My Fair Lady* when they produced the score for another tale of a young girl's coming of age, the 1958 film *Gigi*. Drawn from a novel by the French writer Colette, the movie starred Leslie Caron, all *gamine* charm as the waif who grows into a beautiful woman under the unseeing gaze of Louis Jourdan and grand old man Maurice Chevalier. *Gigi* won a record-breaking nine Oscars, including one for its beguiling title song.

Moderately slow and somewhat freely

from *Gigi*   Words by Alan Jay Lerner; Music by Frederick Loewe

Gi - gi, am I a fool with-out a mind or have I mere-ly been too blind to re-al- ize? Oh, Gi - gi, why you've been grow-ing up be-fore my eyes!

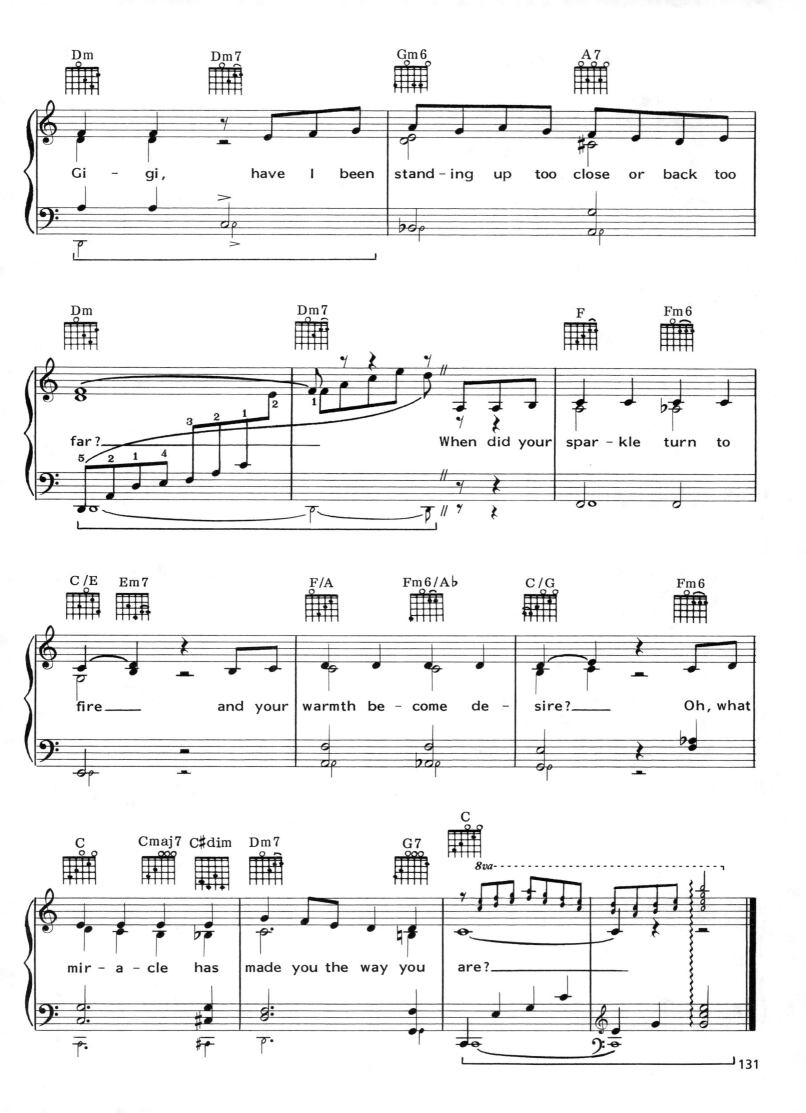

This wistful little song was the centerpiece of *Lili,* the 1953 film that made dancer-turned-actress Leslie Caron a household name for American moviegoers. (Mel Ferrer played the crippled puppeteer who secretly loves the orphaned Lili.) It's said that Helen Deutsch, who wrote the screenplay, was so charmed by Bronislau Kaper's melody that she insisted on writing lyrics to it herself.

from *Lili*   Words by Helen Deutsch; Music by Bronislau Kaper

133

That's Amore

Though his roots were Italian, Harry Warren (born Salvatore Guaragna, in Brooklyn) had never written an expressly "Italian" song when he tackled the job for the 1953 Dean Martin film *The Caddy*. Original plans had called for an old standard of the "Oh, Marie!" type, but Warren insisted he and lyricist Jack Brooks could do better. At 60, with dozens of hits to his credit ("I Found a Million-Dollar Baby," "You'll Never Know," "I Only Have Eyes for You" and "Lullaby of Broadway" among them), he knew what was required, and delivered a ditty that is as Italian as—well, as pizza pie.

from *The Caddy*   Words by Jack Brooks; Music by Harry Warren

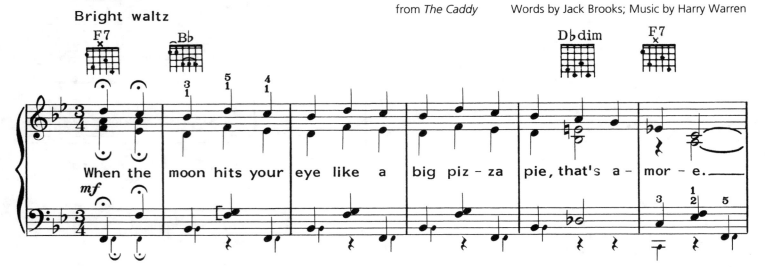

When the moon hits your eye like a big piz-za pie, that's a-mor-e.

When the world seems to shine like you've had too much

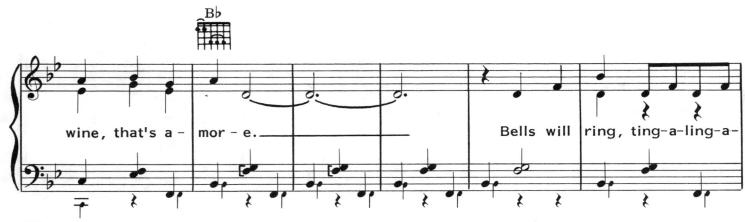

wine, that's a-mor-e. Bells will ring, ting-a-ling-a-

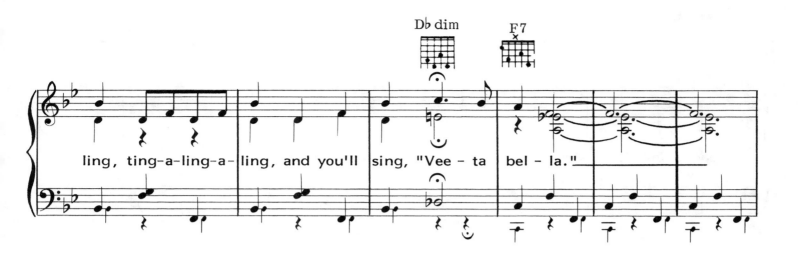

ling, ting-a-ling-a-ling, and you'll sing, "Vee - ta bel - la."

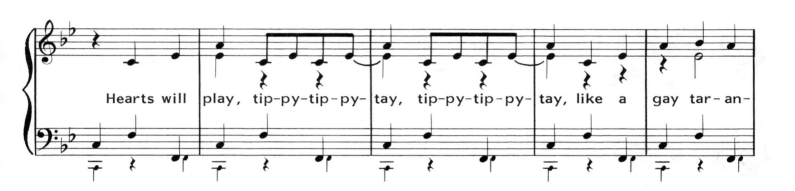

Hearts will play, tip-py-tip-py-tay, tip-py-tip-py-tay, like a gay tar-an-

tel - la,_____ luck-y fel - la. When the stars make you drool just like

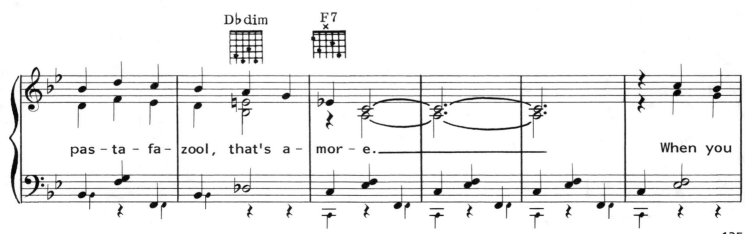

pas - ta - fa - zool, that's a - mor - e._____ When you

The Man That Got Away

Harold Arlen supplied the two songs most closely associated with Judy Garland. She sang his and E.Y. Harburg's "Over the Rainbow" in *The Wizard of Oz* in 1939. Fifteen years later, Arlen and Ira Gershwin wrote this most supreme of torch songs for Judy to sing in the 1954 film *A Star Is Born*. It was her exclusive property ever after.

from *A Star Is Born*   Words by Ira Gershwin; Music by Harold Arlen

Slow and steady

The night is bit - ter, the stars have lost their glit - ter. The winds grow cold - er and sud-den-ly you're old - er. And all be - cause of the {man} {gal} that got a - way. _____ No

141

Around the World

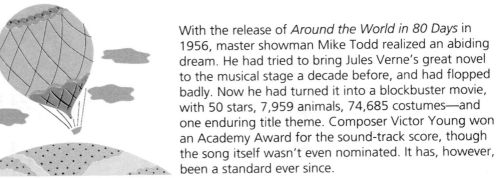

With the release of *Around the World in 80 Days* in 1956, master showman Mike Todd realized an abiding dream. He had tried to bring Jules Verne's great novel to the musical stage a decade before, and had flopped badly. Now he had turned it into a blockbuster movie, with 50 stars, 7,959 animals, 74,685 costumes—and one enduring title theme. Composer Victor Young won an Academy Award for the sound-track score, though the song itself wasn't even nominated. It has, however, been a standard ever since.

from *Around the World in 80 Days*   Words by Harold Adamson; Music by Victor Young

The Loveliest Night of the Year

This was one of tenor Mario Lanza's major hits, first in his 1951 movie, *The Great Caruso* (though he didn't sing it in the film; Ann Blyth, playing Mrs. Caruso, did), and again seven years later in *The Seven Hills of Rome* (when he did). Those with long memories might recognize the melody as "Over the Waves," a waltz imported from Mexico, where it was written in 1888 by Juventino Rosas.

from *The Great Caruso*

Words by Paul Francis Webster; Music by Juventino Rosas, adapted by Irving Aaronson

When you are in love _____ it's the love-li-est night of the year. _____ Stars twin-kle a - bove; _____ and you al-most can touch them from here. _____ Words fall in-to

THE LOVELIEST NIGHT OF THE YEAR

you ____ and the won-der-ful touch of your hand. And

my heart starts to beat ____ like a child when a birth-day is

near. ____ So kiss me, my sweet, ____ it's the

love-li-est night of the year. ____ year. ____

146

I'll Never Stop Loving You

Bright, perky Doris Day seemed an odd choice at first to play the lead in *Love Me or Leave Me,* Hollywood's 1955 screen biography of singer Ruth Etting. But she confounded the nay-sayers by turning in a tough, gritty performance and singing a mixture of standards and newly written songs such as this one with authority and conviction. Nicholas Brodszky, who wrote the melody of "I'll Never Stop Loving You," is perhaps best known for "Be My Love." Lyricist Sammy Cahn, of course, is a four-time Academy Award-winner ("Three Coins in the Fountain," with Jule Styne, and "All the Way," "Call Me Irresponsible" and "High Hopes," all written with Jimmy Van Heusen).

from *Love Me or Leave Me*   Words by Sammy Cahn; Music by Nicholas Brodszky

148

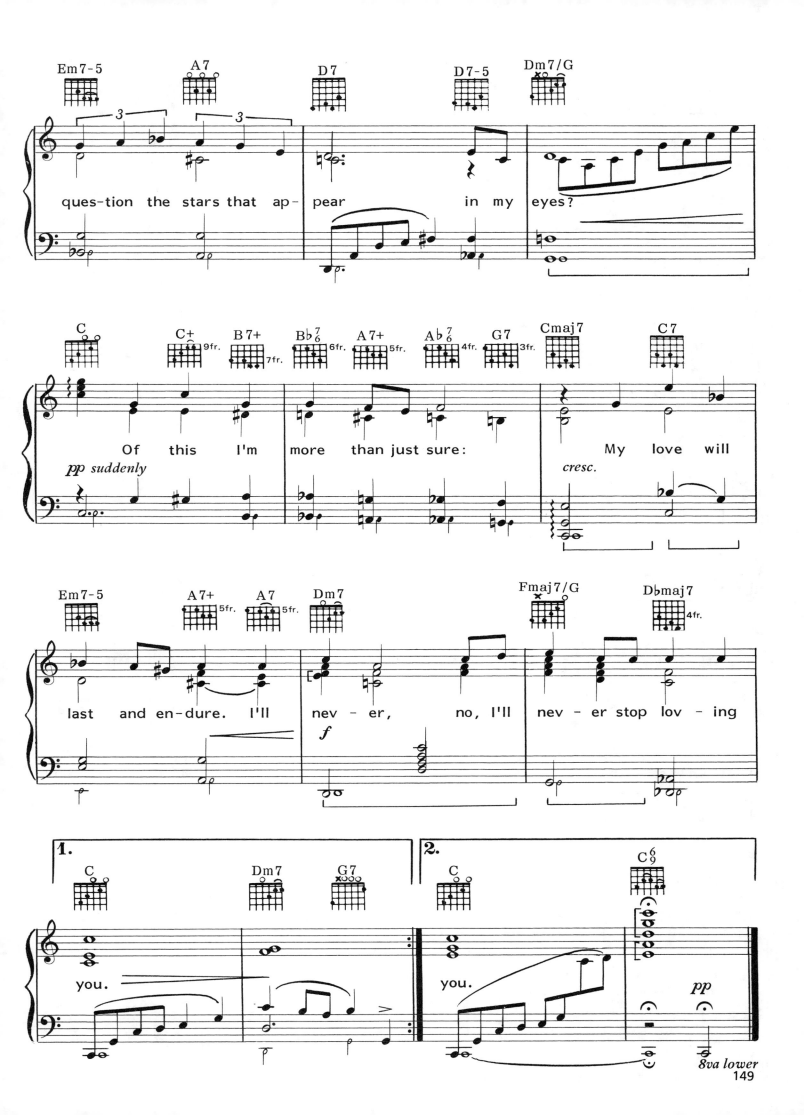

In the Cool, Cool, Cool of the Evening

This Hoagy Carmichael-Johnny Mercer delight had been slated for a Betty Hutton movie, then dropped, when Bing Crosby got wind of it. At Bing's insistence it was slotted into his 1951 film *Here Comes the Groom,* among tunes by Jay Livingston and Ray Evans—and walked off with that year's Oscar as Best Film Song.

from *Here Comes the Groom*   Words by Johnny Mercer; Music by Hoagy Carmichael

With a lilt

mf

Sue wants a bar - be - cue,
"Whee!" said the bum - ble - bee,

Sam wants to boil a ham,
"Let's have a ju - bi - lee."

Grace votes for bouil - la - baisse stew.
"When?" said the prai - rie hen. "Soon?"

Jake wants a wee - ny bake,
"Sure," said the di - no - saur.

steak and a lay - er cake,
"Where?" said the griz - zly bear.

he'll get a tum - my - ache,
"Un - der the light of the

too.
moon?"

ARRIVEDERCI, ROMA

This song of farewell to eternal Rome is indelibly associated with Mario Lanza, the flamboyantly gifted, ill-fated tenor who sang it in the 1958 movie *The Seven Hills of Rome,* a year before his death. Italian musical comedy star Renato Rascel, who played Lanza's cousin in the picture, wrote the bittersweet melody. It seems to echo the adage that Rome is like an old sweetheart, for whom "Goodbye" is just another way of saying "We'll meet again."

English Words by Carl Sigman; Italian Words by Pietro Garinei and Sandro Giovannini; Music by Renato Rascel

ARRIVEDERCI, ROMA

part._____

voir._____

N.C.

Save the wed-ding bells for my re-

Si ri-ve-de a spas-so in car-roz-

turn-ing, keep my lov-er's arms out-stretched and yearn-ing, please be sure the

zel-la, e ri-pen-sa a quel-la "ciu-ma-chel-la" ch'er-a tan-to

flame of love keeps burn-ing in {her}{his} heart._____

bel-la e che gli ha det-to sem-pre "No!"_____ Ar-

Ar-

ri - ve - der - ci, Ro - ma!_____

ri - ve - der - ci, Ro - ma!_____

VOLARE

(Nel Blu, Dipinto di Blu)

This Italian import made the charts twice in two years, under two different names. As "Nel Blu, Dipinto di Blu," sung by its Sicilian co-lyricist Domenico Modugno, it won first prize at the San Remo Song Festival and a Grammy as 1958 song of the year. Then, with an English text (by "Star Dust" lyricist Mitchell Parish) and retitled "Volare," it hit the top again, thanks to a 1960 recording by Bobby Rydell.

Italian Words by Domenico Modugno and Francesco Migliacci;
English Words by Mitchell Parish; Music by Domenico Modugno

Ad lib – in 2 (♩=1 beat)

Guitar tacet till chorus.

VOLARE (NEL BLU, DIPINTO DI BLU)

Oh! My Papa

This typically German *Schlager*, or sentimental pop song, first surfaced as "O Mein Papa" in a late '40s Swiss musical film called *Fireworks*. English trumpeter Eddie Calvert heard it while on a European tour and recorded it as an instrumental. It did well enough to alert record executives on this side of the Atlantic. Eddie Fisher recorded an English-language version in 1953, adding another million-seller to a list that included "Any Time," "Wish You Were Here" and "I Need You Now."

English Words by John Turner and Geoffrey Parsons;
German Words and Music by Paul Burkhard

Moderately slow, in 2 (♩ = 1 beat)

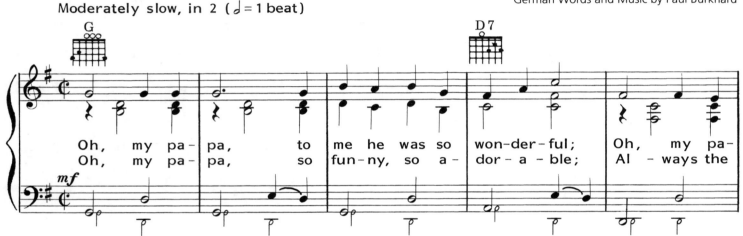

Oh, my pa-pa, to me he was so won-der-ful; Oh, my pa-
Oh, my pa-pa, so fun-ny, so a-dor-a-ble; Al - ways the

pa, to me he was so good. No one could be so
clown, so fun-ny in his way. Oh, my pa-pa, to

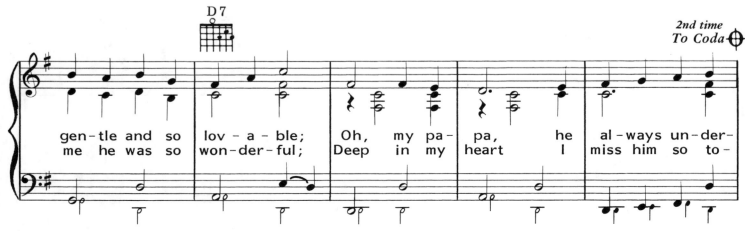

2nd time
To Coda ⊕

gen-tle and so lov-a-ble; Oh, my pa-pa, he al-ways un-der-
me he was so won-der-ful; Deep in my heart I miss him so to-

IF YOU LOVE ME
(Really Love Me)
(Hymne á l'amour)

"Hymne á l'amour" ("Hymn to Love") was the French title of this compelling song. It was composed for Edith Piaf, who wrote the French text; and, as only she could do, the incomparable Little Sparrow left her imprint on it forever. Piaf died in 1963, but the quality of her voice—its urgency, vulnerability and pain—makes her a living presence even now to all who hear her recordings, a presence still evoked strongly here in both melody and words.

English Words by Geoffrey Parsons; French Words by Edith Piaf; Music by Marguerite Monnot

If the sun should tum-ble from the sky, if the
Le ciel bleu sur nous peut s'é-crou-ler, et la

sea should sud-den-ly run dry, if you love me, real-ly
ter-re peut bien s'ef-fon-drer. Peu m'im-por-te, si tu

love me, let it hap-pen, I won't care. If it
m'ai - mes, je me moque du monde en - tier. Tant qu'l'a-

seems that ev-'ry-thing is lost, I will smile and nev-er count the
mour i - non-dra mes ma - tins, que mon corps fré - mi - ra sous tes

cost. If you love me, real - ly love me, let it
mains, peu m'im- porte les grands pro - blè - mes, mon a -

hap-pen, dar - ling, I won't care._____ Shall I
mour, puis - que tu m'ai - mes._____ J'i - rais

freely and

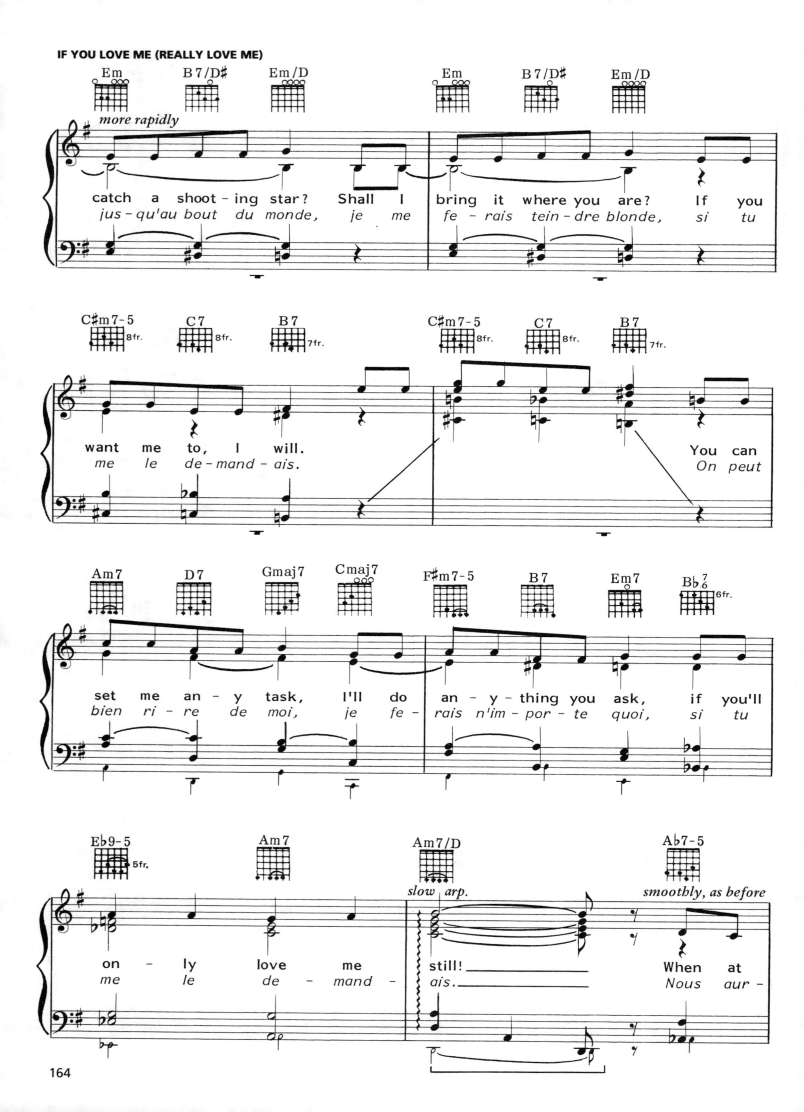

IF YOU LOVE ME (REALLY LOVE ME)

last   our life on earth is | through,   I will
ons   pour nous l'é - ter - ni - | té   dans le

share   e - ter - ni - ty with | you.   If you love me, real - ly
bleu   de toute l'im-men-si - | té.   Dans le ciel plus de pro-

love me,   then what - | ev - er   hap - pens   I   won't
blè - mes,   Dieu ré - | u - nit   ceux qui   s'ai -

1.
care.   If the
ment.   Le ciel

2.
care.
ment.

165

Answer Me, My Love

Fewer of our popular song hits have been imported from Germany or Austria than from England or France, but several have been memorable. These songs range from "When Day Is Done" in the 1920s and "Falling in Love Again," as popularized by Marlene Dietrich, to this 1954 favorite, written in Germany as "Mutterlein" ("Mother Love"), and sung so unforgettably by Nat King Cole.

English Words by Carl Sigman; Original German Words by Fred Rauch; Music by Gerhard Winkler

Moderate gentle waltz

An-swer me, oh my love; Just what sin have I been guilt-y of?

Tell me how I came to lose your love. Please an-swer me, my love.

You were mine yes-ter-day; I be-lieved that love was here to stay.

AUTUMN LEAVES

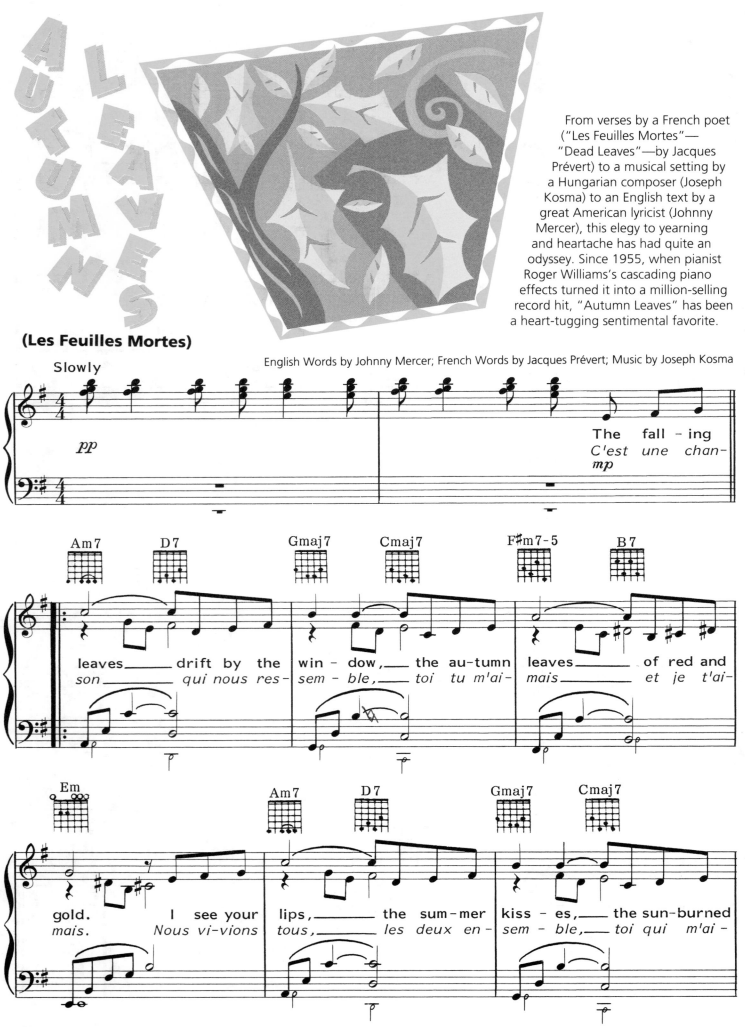

From verses by a French poet ("Les Feuilles Mortes"— "Dead Leaves"—by Jacques Prévert) to a musical setting by a Hungarian composer (Joseph Kosma) to an English text by a great American lyricist (Johnny Mercer), this elegy to yearning and heartache has had quite an odyssey. Since 1955, when pianist Roger Williams's cascading piano effects turned it into a million-selling record hit, "Autumn Leaves" has been a heart-tugging sentimental favorite.

(Les Feuilles Mortes)

English Words by Johnny Mercer; French Words by Jacques Prévert; Music by Joseph Kosma

I Get Ideas

This good-natured invitation to dalliance on the dance floor is actually just the eternally popular Argentine tango "Adios Muchachos" ("Good-bye Boys"), tricked out in new finery by dancer-turned-lyricist Dorcas Cochran. Singer Tony Martin had the big record, in 1950. Louis Armstrong also afforded the song his own unique vocal treatment on the flip side of his 1951 hit "A Kiss to Build a Dream On."

English Words by Dorcas Cochran; Music by Julio C. Sanders

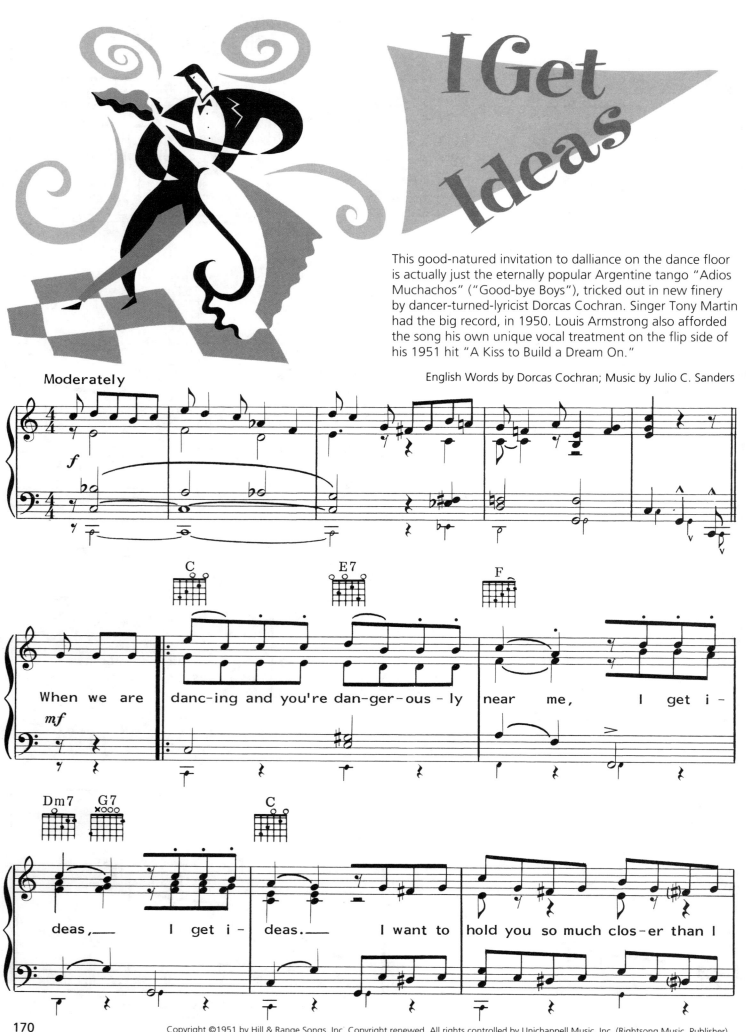

Moderately

When we are dancing and you're danger-ous-ly near me, I get i-deas, I get i-deas. I want to hold you so much clos-er than I

I GET IDEAS

172

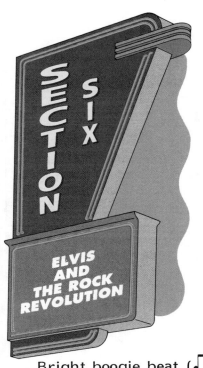

SHAKE, RATTLE AND ROLL

In several ways, Bill Haley could be called the father of rock and roll. In 1953, his "Crazy Man Crazy," with The Comets, became the first rock song to hit the pop charts, and two years later "Rock Around the Clock" became the first rock record to make it all the way to No.1. In addition, it was the lyrics of his song "Rock-a-Beatin' Boogie" that supposedly inspired disc jockey Alan Freed to coin the term "rock and roll." "Shake, Rattle and Roll" joined "Rock Around the Clock" in the Top 10 in 1955. It had been a giant hit in the rhythm-and-blues market for blues shouter Big Joe Turner. The lyrics were cleaned up a little for Bill, but the song's message came through loud and clear: A revolution in music was at hand.

Words and Music by Charles Calhoun

* *More skillful players should play all notes, large and small. For easier version play large notes only.*

173

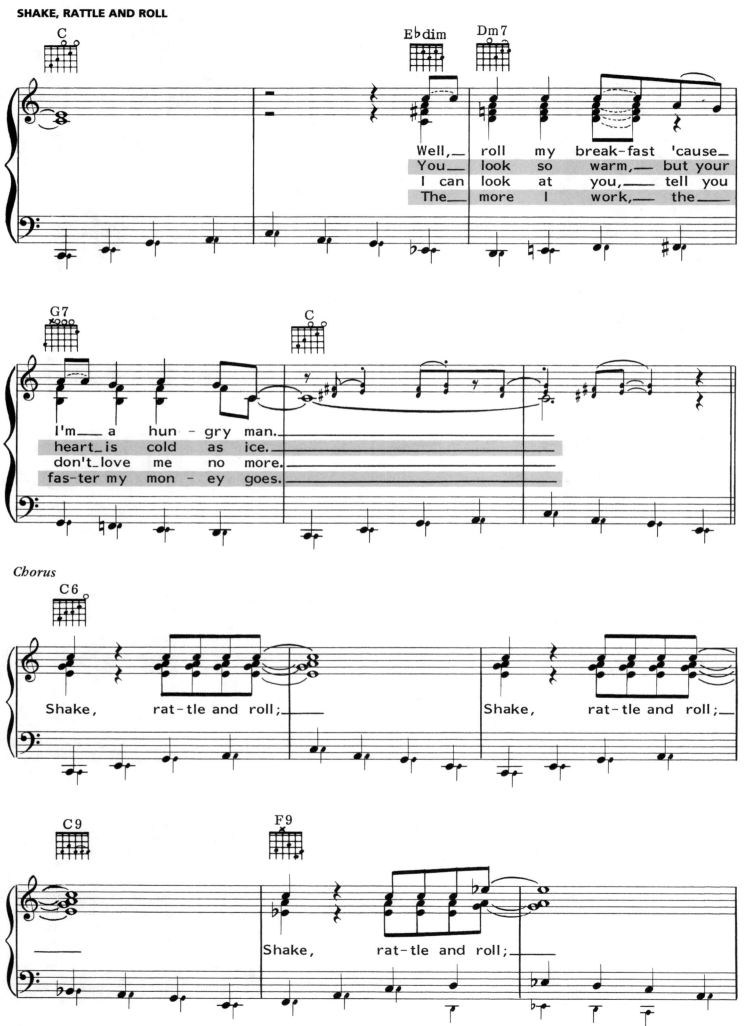

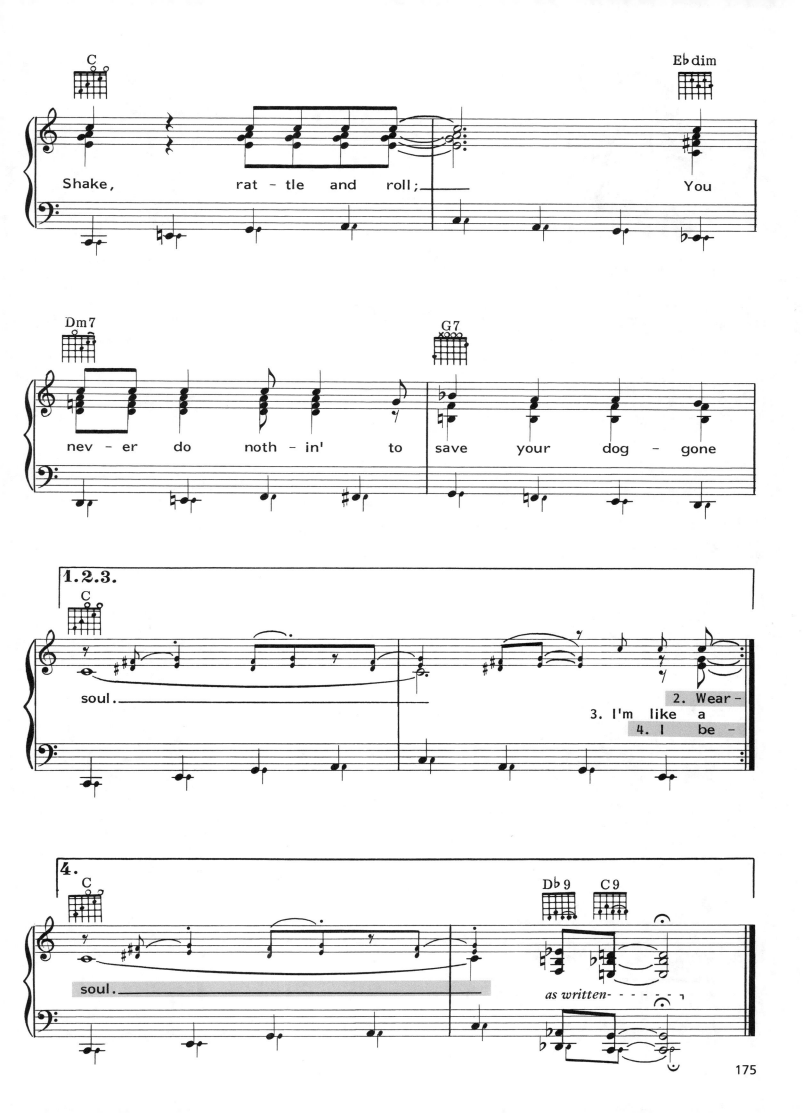

In the mid-'50s, Elvis Presley's recording of
"Hound Dog" was a shot heard round the
world. Nothing would ever be the same
again: Elvis was on the scene, and rock
and roll was here to stay. The song
is the work of Jerry Leiber and Mike
Stoller, who have written many
of the great rock-and-roll hits,
including—for Elvis alone—
"Love Me," "Loving You,"
"Treat Me Nice," "Jailhouse
Rock," "Don't" and "King Creole."

Words and Music by Jerry Leiber and Mike Stoller

I Want You, I Need You, I Love You

As all his fans know, with Elvis it wasn't all rocking; he had a softer side that came out in sentimental ballads like this 1956 effort by Maurice Mysels and Ira Kosloff. He sang it in July of that year on *The Steve Allen Show* dressed in white tie and tails—and far from looking foolish, as the show's producers seem to have hoped, he came across as dignified and quite tender. "I Want You" made the Top 10 country, rhythm-and-blues and pop charts and sold another easy million for the man who was soon to become known as The King of Rock and Roll, and then, simply, as The King.

Words by Maurice Mysels; Music by Ira Kosloff

Slow rock and roll

Hold me close,___ hold me tight,___ make me thrill___ with de-light,_____ let me know___ where I stand___ from the start. I want you, I need you, I

love you___ with all my heart.___ Ev-'ry

time___ that you're near___ all my cares___ dis-ap-pear.___ Dar-ling,

you're___ all that I'm___ liv-ing for.___ I want you, I need you, I

love you___ more and more.___ I

LOVE ME TENDER

In addition to being the title song of Elvis Presley's first motion picture, "Love Me Tender" was the first great "straight" love song of his career. His recording reached the Top 5 on all three charts—pop, country, and rhythm and blues—when it was released in September 1956. The soft and touching tune, credited to Elvis and Vera Matson, is based on the 1861 ballad "Aura Lea," in keeping with the movie's Civil War theme.

Moderately slow

Words and Music by Elvis Presley and Vera Matson

1. Love me ten-der, love me sweet; Nev-er let me go.
2. Love me ten-der, love me long; Take me to your heart.
3. Love me ten-der, love me dear; Tell me you are mine.

You have made my life com-plete, and I love you so.
For it's there that I be-long, and we'll nev-er part.
I'll be yours through all the years, till the end of time.

(Let Me Be Your) TEDDY BEAR

Rock-and-roll trivia buffs take note: In the scene in Elvis Presley's second film, *Loving You*, where he sings this song, sharp eyes will catch his mother sitting in the third row of the audience, beaming proudly. Elvis got "Teddy Bear" from Bernie Lowe and Kal Mann, the same team that later wrote "The Twist" for Chubby Checker, launching an international craze. Predictably, when "Teddy Bear" hit the charts (it was one of four Presley recordings that reached No.1 on the pop, country *and* rhythm-and-blues playlists), Elvis was inundated with stuffed animals mailed to him by fans; most of the stuffed toys were sent on to charity.

Words and Music by Bernie Lowe and Kal Mann

Baby, let me be____ your lov-in' ted-dy bear.____
Baby, let me be____ a-round you ev-'ry night.____

Put a chain a-round my neck____ and lead me an-y-where.____
Run your fin-gers through my hair____ and cud-dle me real tight.____
Oh, let me

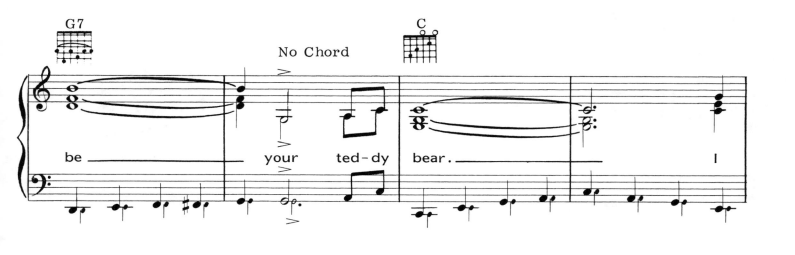

be _____ your ted-dy bear. _____ I

don't want to be your ti - ger 'cause ti - gers play too rough. I

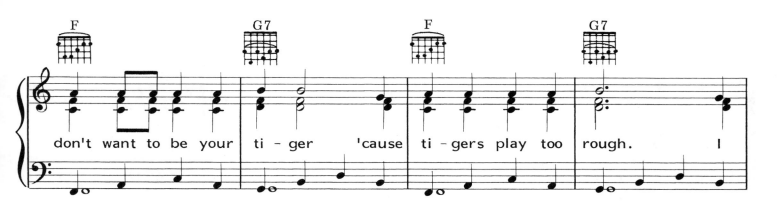

don't want to be your li - on, 'cause li - ons ain't the kind you love e-

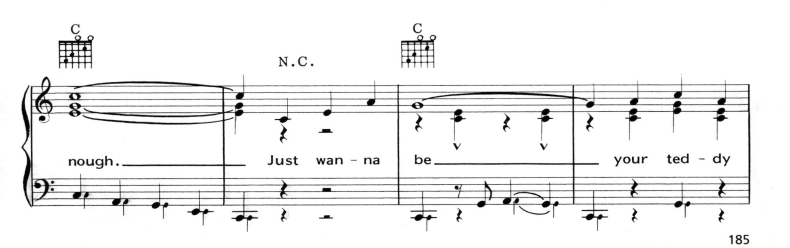

nough. _____ Just wan - na be _____ your ted - dy

This was Elvis Presley's biggest hit. The 1956 single ("Hound Dog" was on the other side) sold nine million copies, and was the first record ever to reach No.1 on *Billboard* magazine's three charts—pop, country and rhythm-and-blues. ("All Shook Up," "Teddy Bear" and "Jailhouse Rock" were soon to reach that illustrious position.) Another milestone for Elvis: "Don't Be Cruel" and "Hound Dog" marked the only time that both sides of a single record made No.1 separately.

Don't Be Cruel
(to a Heart That's True)

Words and Music by Otis Blackwell and Elvis Presley

Bright rock beat

You know I can be found sit-ting home all a-lone. If you can't come a-round, at least please tel-e-phone. Don't be cruel_____ to a heart that's true._____

DON'T BE CRUEL (TO A HEART THAT'S TRUE)

188

JAILHOUSE ROCK

"Jailhouse Rock" is another fine Leiber-Stoller composition, another movie title song and, needless to say, another No.1 hit and million-seller for Elvis Presley, in 1957. It may have been Jerry Leiber or it may have been Mike Stoller who said, "We don't write songs, we write records." Whatever ... it said a lot about the complex editing and dubbing process that helped turn their efforts with Elvis, The Coasters and others into hits. But obviously these two also had a knack for writing songs that, like their chief client, found the pulse of the public.

Words and Music by Jerry Leiber and Mike Stoller

Medium rock and roll

1. The war-den threw a par-ty in the coun-ty jail;___ The
2. Spi-der Mur-phy played the ten-or sax-o-phone,___ ___
(3. The) sad sack was a-sit-tin' on a block of stone,___ way
4. Shift-y Hen-ry said to Bugs, "For heav-en's sake,___ ___

pris-on band was there and they be-gan to wail.___ The
Lit-tle Joe was blow-in' on the slide trom-bone.___ The
o-ver in the cor-ner weep-in' all a-lone.___ The
no one's look-in'; Now's our chance to make a break."___ ___

band was jump-in' and the joint be-gan to swing.___ You
drum-mer boy from Il-li-nois went crash, boom, bang;___ The
war-den said, "Hey, bud-dy, don't you be no square.___ If
Bug-sy turned to Shift-y and he said, "Nix, nix;___ I

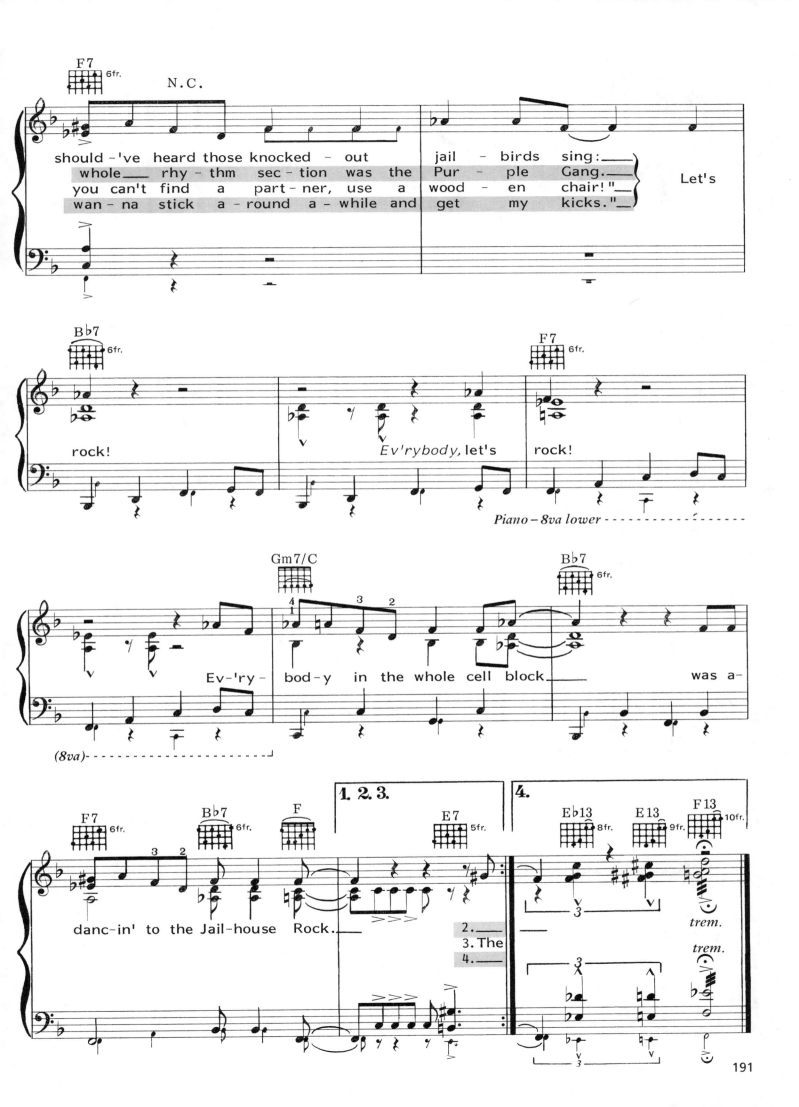

Before his death in the 1959 plane crash that also killed Buddy Holly and The Big Bopper, J.P. Richardson, 19-year-old Ritchie Valens had secured his place as the first Chicano rock star. He had turned this old Mexican folk song into a hit—though the flip side, "Donna," named after his girlfriend, actually ranked higher on the charts. Valens's fame—and that of "La Bamba"—became even greater after the release of the 1987 film biography of the singer, called *La Bamba*.

Adaptation and Arrangement by Ritchie Valens

With a strong Latin beat

Pa-ra bai-lar___ la Bam - ba,   pa-ra bai-lar___ la Bam-

- ba se ne-ce-si - ta un a po-ca de gra-cia.

To Coda ⊕

193

LA BAMBA

Peggy Sue

Texas-born Buddy Holly was the first to fuse the sound and flavor of country music with a heavy backbeat borrowed from black rhythm and blues. The result was a dynamic new sound, typified by such songs as "Peggy Sue," as well as "That'll Be the Day," "It Doesn't Matter Anymore" and "Maybe Baby." When Buddy died in a plane crash on February 3, 1959, many people felt that rock and roll died with him. (Among them was Don McLean, who years later wrote "American Pie" about the death of Holly, Ritchie Valens and The Big Bopper.) But rock and roll is still alive and well, and Holly is still a strong musical influence—as evidenced by the 1990 musical of his life, *Buddy*.

Bright rock and roll (in 2, ♩ = 1 beat)

Words and Music by Jerry Allison, Norman Petty and Buddy Holly

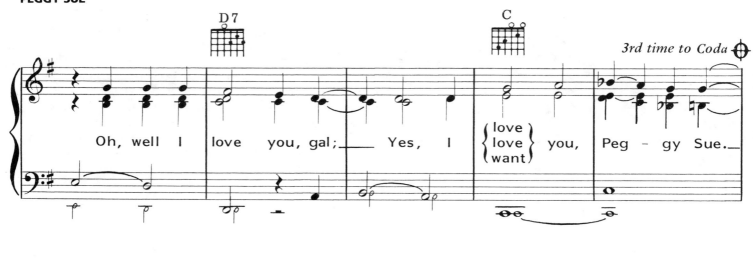

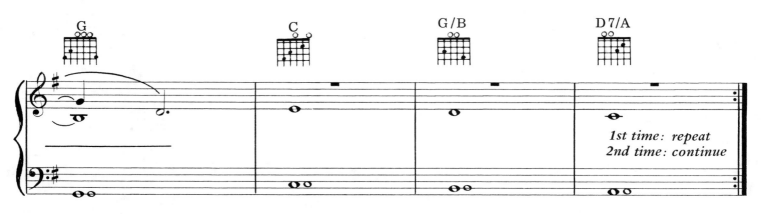

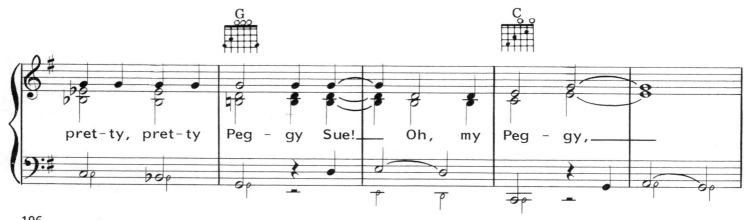

ROCK AROUND THE CLOCK

Now it's hard to believe, but Bill Haley and His Comets' "Rock Around the Clock" went almost unnoticed when the recording was released in the spring of 1954. A year later the song was featured on the sound track of *The Blackboard Jungle,* a movie that starred Glenn Ford as a city high-school teacher fighting back against juvenile delinquency. The re-released single became a sensation, selling millions of copies and becoming the first rock-and-roll record to reach No.1 on the hit parade.

Moderate boogie-rock beat

Words and Music by Max C. Freedman and Jimmy De Knight

One, two, three o'-clock, four o'-clock rock! Five, six, sev-en o'-clock, eight o'-clock rock! Nine, ten, e-lev-en o'-clock, twelve o'-clock rock! We're gon-na rock a-round the clock to-night!_ Put your

(1) glad rags on and join me, hon,__ we'll have some fun when the
(2) clock strikes two and three and four,__ if the band slows down, we'll__
(3) chimes ring five and six and seven,_ we'll be rock-in' up in__
(4) eight, nine, ten, e-lev-en, too,__ I'll be go-in' strong and__
(5) clock strikes twelve, we'll cool off then _ start a-rock-in' 'round the

Bye Bye, Love

This rockabilly lament penned by husband-and-wife songwriters Boudleaux and Felice Bryant meant stardom for The Everly Brothers. Sons of country singers Ike and Margaret Everly, Don and Phil grew up on the road, singing and playing guitar at clubs and on radio stations throughout the South and Midwest. "Bye Bye, Love," in May 1957, was their big breakthrough, followed by such other tuneful Bryant collaborations as "Wake Up, Little Susie," "Bird Dog" and "All I Have to Do Is Dream."

Words and Music by Felice Bryant and Boudleaux Bryant

There goes my ba - by _____ with some - one
(I'm through with) ro - mance, _____ I'm through with

new. _____ She sure looks hap - py;
love. _____ I'm through with count - ing

I sure am blue. _____ She was my
the stars a - bove. _____ And here's the

Charlie Brown

Nothing to do with Peanuts and Lucy here, folks: *this* Charlie Brown is a cool dude who strolls through life unfazed by anything. This 1959 tune is one of the songs of protest and sly satire that Jerry Leiber and Mike Stoller were turning out in the late '50s and that their protégés The Coasters were turning into best-sellers on both the pop and rhythm-and-blues charts. Other Coasters classics include the two-sided hit "Searching" and "Young Blood," "Yakety Yak" and "Along Came Jones."

Medium bright rock *(8th notes played evenly)*

Words and Music by Jerry Leiber and Mike Stoller

NIGHT TRAIN

It all started with Duke Ellington, who stitched this simple, insistent blues theme into his 1946 concert suite *Happy-Go-Lucky Local*. The railroad association clearly stuck in the mind of tenor saxophonist Jimmy Forrest, who worked with Ellington in 1949–50. After leaving the Duke, he developed the tune as a rhythm-and-blues specialty. Bandleader Buddy Morrow picked it up, and eventually it gained a lyric. The result: an enduring hit—but one not credited to Ellington.

Words by Oscar D. Washington and Lewis E. Simpkins; Music by Jimmy Forrest

Slow boogie-blues

Note: Organ pedal doubles lowest note of piano left hand throughout.

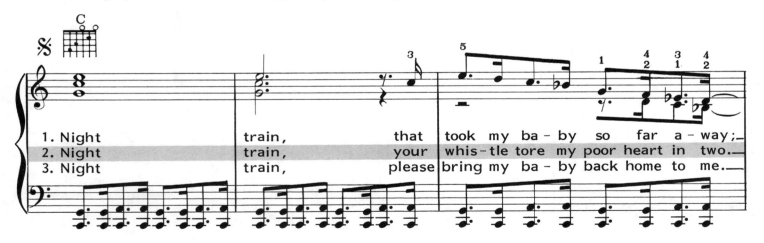

1. Night train, that took my ba-by so far a-way;
2. Night train, your whis-tle tore my poor heart in two.
3. Night train, please bring my ba-by back home to me.

Night train, that
Night train, your
Night train, please

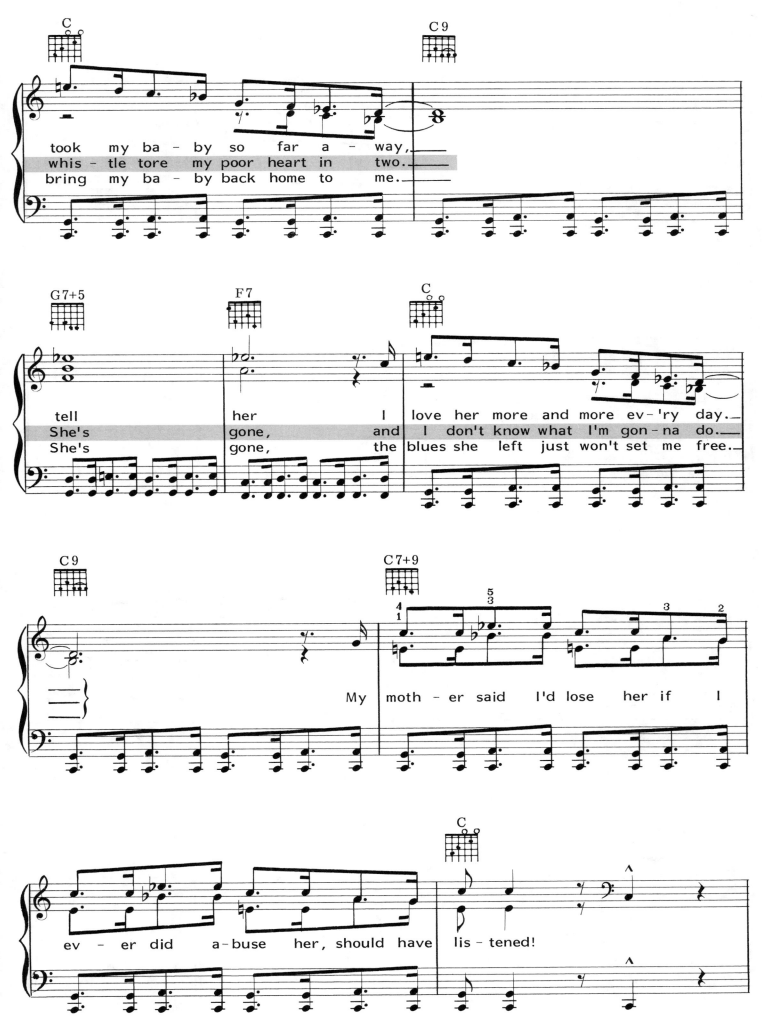

took my ba – by so far a – way,
whis – tle tore my poor heart in two.
bring my ba – by back home to me.

tell her I love her more and more ev – 'ry day.
She's gone, and I don't know what I'm gon – na do.
She's gone, the blues she left just won't set me free.

My moth – er said I'd lose her if I

ev – er did a – buse her, should have lis – tened!

My | moth – er said I'd lose her if I

ev – er did a–buse her, should have | lis – tened!

Now I have learned my les – son, my sweet

ba – by was a bless – ing, should have | lis – tened!

D. S. %

208

Great Balls of Fire

Jerry Lee Lewis, born in Ferriday, Louisiana, began his career at Sun Records in Memphis, where Elvis Presley also started out. "Whole Lotta Shakin' Goin' On," his first hit in the summer of 1957, was followed by "Great Balls of Fire," which became No. 1 in both the country and pop fields. A lackluster decade with few hits followed, and Jerry Lee turned away from the rock and roll that had made him a teenage idol and went back to his country roots. *Great Balls of Fire* was the title of a 1989 movie depicting "The Killer's" flamboyant life.

Bright rock tempo

Words and Music by Otis Blackwell and Jack Hammer

You shake my nerves and you rat-tle my brain;—
Too much love drives a man in-sane.— You broke my will,
but what a thrill; Good-ness, gra-cious, great balls of fire!—
I laughed at love 'cause I thought it was fun-ny;

*piano only

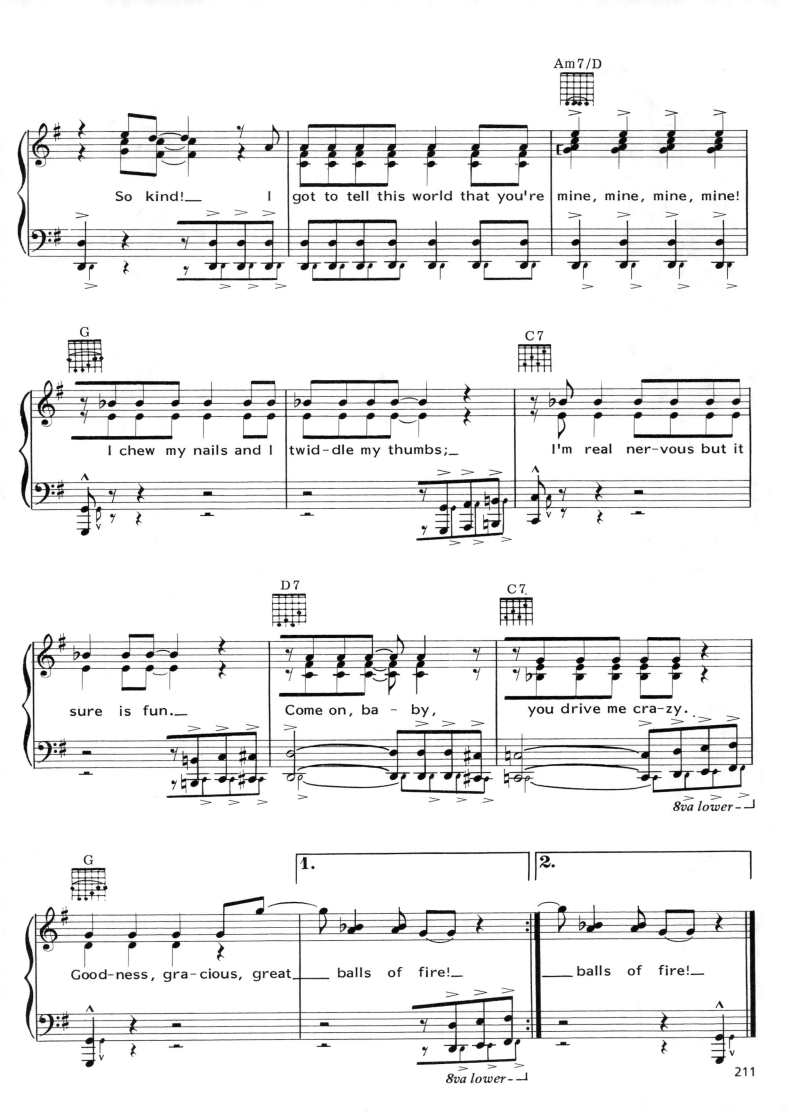

So kind!__ I got to tell this world that you're mine, mine, mine, mine!

I chew my nails and I twid-dle my thumbs;__ I'm real ner-vous but it

sure is fun.__ Come on, ba - by, you drive me cra-zy.

8va lower

1. Good-ness, gra-cious, great__ balls of fire!__

2. __balls of fire!__

8va lower

YOUR CHEATIN' HEART

Hank Williams' rise was meteoric; his end—from a heart attack, in the back seat of a car en route to an appearance in West Virginia—tragic. In between came alcoholism, drug addiction—and some of the most beautiful of all country songs. "Your Cheatin' Heart," like "Cold, Cold Heart," reportedly grew out of his constant domestic troubles. Issued in January 1953, just after Hank's death, the recording became his ninth million-seller. The song has been recorded by more than 100 artists since then.

SECTION SEVEN

COUNTRY-STYLE CROSSOVER HITS

Words and Music by Hank Williams

Moderate country tempo

Your cheat-in'

heart _____ will make you weep. _____ You'll cry and _____
heart _____ will pine some- day _____ and crave the _____

cry _____ and try to sleep. _____ But sleep won't _____
love _____ you threw a- way. _____ The time will _____

YOUR CHEATIN' HEART

214

Eddy Arnold was probably the first country performer to "cross over" successfully into the pop market. Starting with such million-sellers as "I'll Hold You in My Heart (Till I Can Hold You in My Arms)," "Any Time" and "Bouquet of Roses" in the late 1940s, he proved that a relaxed, easygoing approach to a song would appeal to any audience. This lover's confession, which he co-authored with Cindy Walker in 1955, turned out to be one of the Tennessee Plowboy's major successes.

You Don't Know Me

Words and Music by Cindy Walker and Eddy Arnold

You give your hand to me and then you say, "Hel-lo," and I can hard-ly speak, my heart is beat-ing so. And an-y-one could tell you think you know me well, but you don't know me. No, you don't

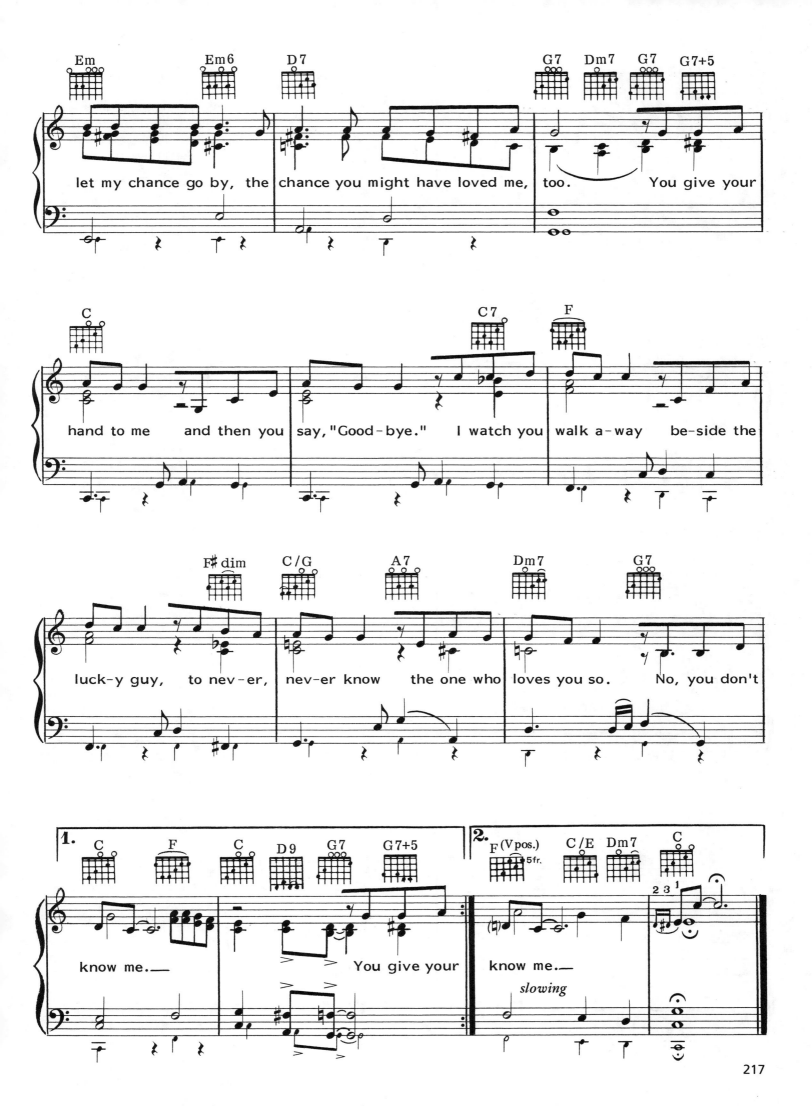

I Almost Lost My Mind

"I Almost Lost My Mind" is a turnabout, a rhythm-and-blues hit "borrowed" successfully by the country market instead of the other way around. Blues singer-pianist Ivory Joe Hunter wrote the song in 1950, inspired by a Nashville friend named Martha Spencer, whose husband had left her. When Hunter heard the story, he said, "I went right to the piano, and the whole song came to me all at once." Pat Boone, who covered many other R&B songs, had a No. 1 hit with Hunter's tune in 1956.

Words and Music by Ivory Joe Hunter

Slow blues

When I lost my ba - by,__ I al - most_ lost__ my mind.__
pass a mil - lion peo - ple,__ I can't tell__ who__ I meet.
went to see a gyp - sy,__ and had__ my__ for - tune read.
I can tell you, peo - ple, the news_ was__ not__ so good.

Opt. fill in

When I lost my ba - by,__ I
I pass a mil - lion peo - ple,__ I
I went to see a gyp - sy,__ and
I can tell you, peo - ple, the

Three guys named Eddie figured in the success of this lilting love song, which was around nearly 30 years before becoming a hit. Country singer Eddy Arnold spotted and recorded it in 1948, turning it into a million-seller. But it took 23-year-old Eddie Fisher, protégé of the great comedian Eddie Cantor, to hit the big money—and No. 2 on the charts—with a pop version of the song, in 1951. "Any Time" made Fisher a star, and remained his trademark for years to come.

Words and Music by Herbert "Happy" Lawson

Now wait just a minute: a song called "Tennessee Waltz," about a song called "Tennessee Waltz"? Curious—though none of the 6 million people who bought Patti Page's hit 1950 record seemed unduly bothered by the apparent illogicality. Written by *Grand Ole Opry* stars Pee Wee King and Redd Stewart (after they heard the "Kentucky Waltz" on the radio), it became Tennessee's official song in 1965.

Words and Music by Pee Wee King and Redd Stewart

Crying in the Chapel

Such widely dissimilar performers as pop singer June Valli, cowboy movie star Rex Allen, and The Orioles, one of the first of the black rhythm-and-blues vocal groups of the '50s, tackled this country weeper on records in 1953. All did well—but it took Elvis Presley's 1965 recording to nudge the song all the way into the best-seller class.

Words and Music by Artie Glenn

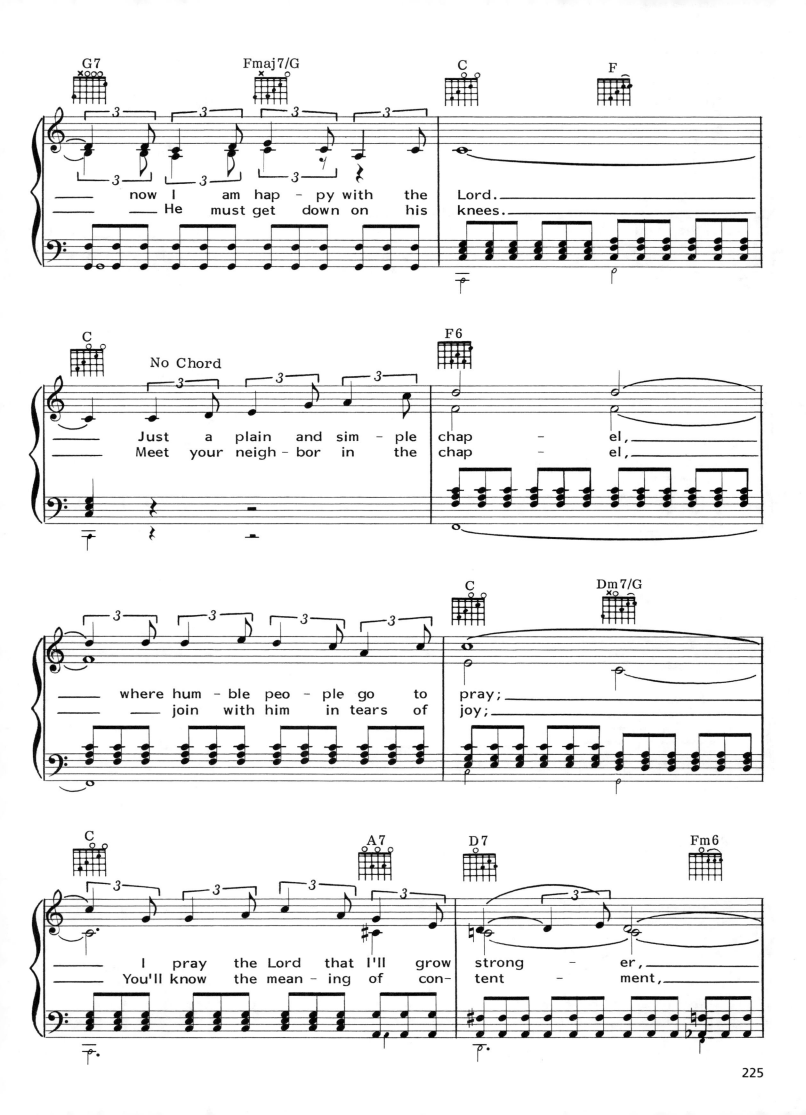

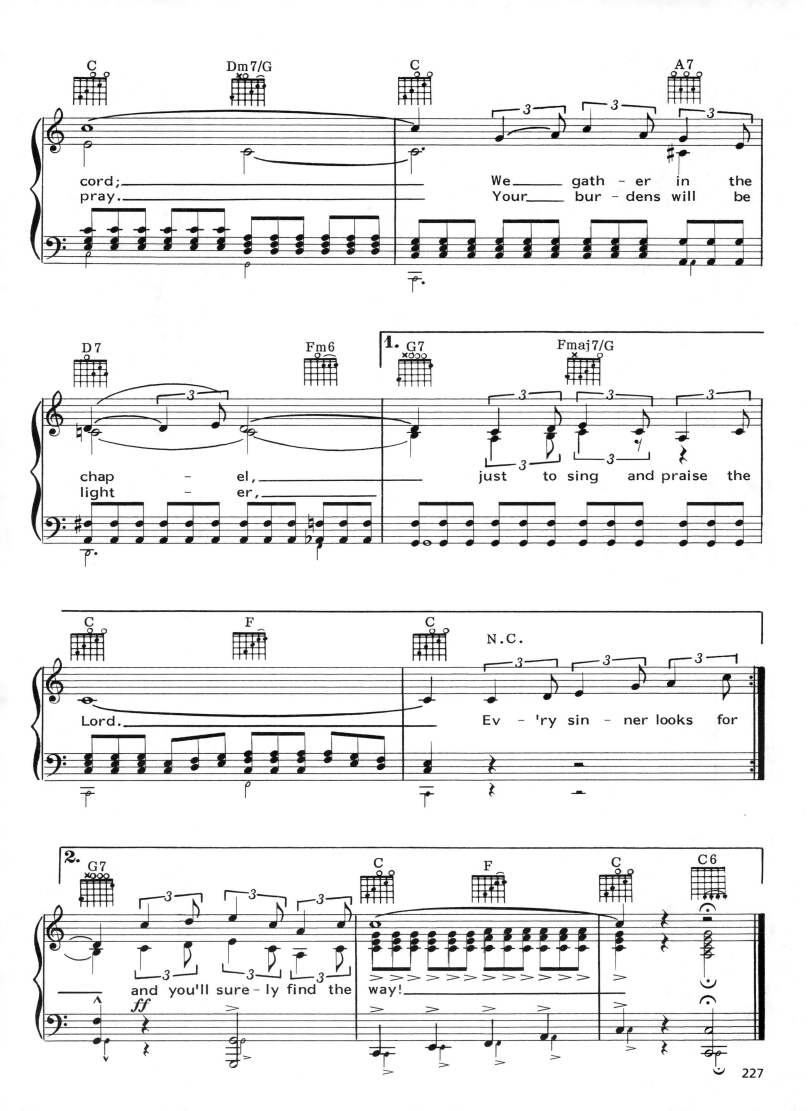

COLD, COLD HEART

Singer-songwriter Hank Williams was one of the great troubadours of modern times, the man who brought country music into the pop mainstream. Complex and vulnerable, he seemed to reach within himself for the emotions that drove such songs as "Your Cheatin' Heart," "I'm So Lonesome I Could Cry" and "I'll Never Get Out of This World Alive." He wrote "Cold, Cold Heart" in 1951 after a quarrel with his wife. It became his most successful song and his personal favorite. Williams died at 29, in 1953.

Words and Music by Hank Williams

Medium country beat

tried so hard, my dear, to show that you're my ev-'ry dream. Yet
nev-er know how much it hurts to see you sit and cry. You

you're a-fraid each thing I do is just some e-vil scheme. A
know you need and want my love, yet you're a-fraid to try. Why

mem-'ry from your lone-some past keeps us so far a-part.
do you run and hide from life? To try it just ain't smart. Why

can't I free your doubt-ful mind and melt your cold, cold heart? An-
There

oth-er love be-fore my time made your heart sad and blue, and
was a time when I be-lieved that you be-longed to me, but

so my heart is pay-ing now for things I did-n't do. In
now I know your heart is shack-led to a mem-o-ry. The

Optional: For variety, pianists may play the melody an 8va higher till the end.

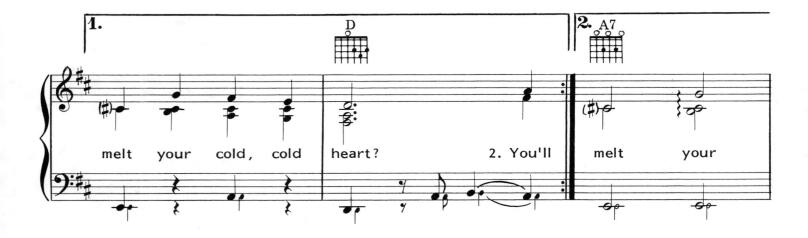

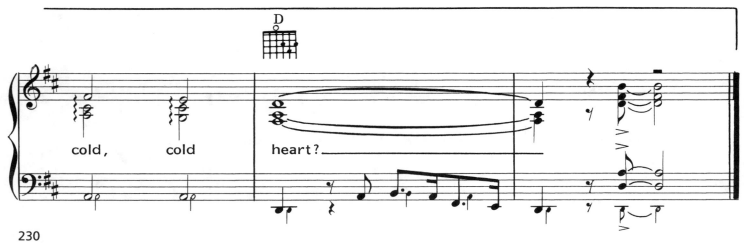

Blue Velvet

Tony Bennett first came to prominence in June of 1951 with "Because of You" and within a few years had put eight other songs on the charts. One of these was "Blue Velvet"—*the* romantic song for many teenagers growing up in the decade. Bobby Vinton had an even bigger hit with the tune in 1963. And the song's staying power was certified when it lent its title to director David Lynch's 1986 cult classic film *Blue Velvet*.

Words and Music by Bernie Wayne and Lee Morris

Slowly

She wore blue vel-vet. Blu-er than vel-vet was the night, soft-er than sat-in was the light from the stars. She wore blue vel-vet.

ONLY YOU

The Platters had an overnight hit with this Buck Ram ballad in 1955—and with it a major music industry breakthrough. Before The Platters, all-black vocal groups, even The Ink Spots, refined their sound to make it more acceptable to the mostly white mass audience. Now, for the first time, a group sounded unabashedly and authentically black. With this hit and others, such as "My Prayer," "Smoke Gets In Your Eyes" and "(You've Got) The Magic Touch," The Platters—four men and a teenage girl—became one of the top groups in pop music history.

Slow rock and roll tempo

Words and Music by Buck Ram and Ande Rand

Why Don't You Believe Me

Remember when female pop singers all seemed to have alliterative names? Gogi Grant, Kitty Kallen, Patti Page—and a petite Chicago lass named Joni James. Born Joan Carmello Babbo, Joni started as a dancer, switched to singing and hit No. 1 in 1952 with this teary ballad. She followed it with such other romantic teen hits as "Have You Heard?" and her version of Hank Williams' "Your Cheatin' Heart."

Words and Music by Lew Douglas, Roy Rodde and King Laney

Moderately slow

Why don't you be-lieve me? It's you I a-dore for-ev-er and ev-er. Can I prom-ise

The Great Pretender

The first association here, of course, is with the vocal stylings of The Platters—Tony Williams, Herbert Reed, David Lynch, Paul Robi and Zola Taylor (who first joined the group on this recording). But the creative force behind both the group and this, their greatest hit, was the versatile Buck Ram. Saxophonist, arranger, songwriter, agent and talent scout, Ram had worked for everybody, had helped discover Ella Fitzgerald and Maxine Sullivan and had sold both The Platters and The Penguins to Mercury Records. He also wrote two other Platters successes, "Only You" (see page 234) and "Twilight Time."

Words and Music by Buck Ram

THE GREAT PRETENDER

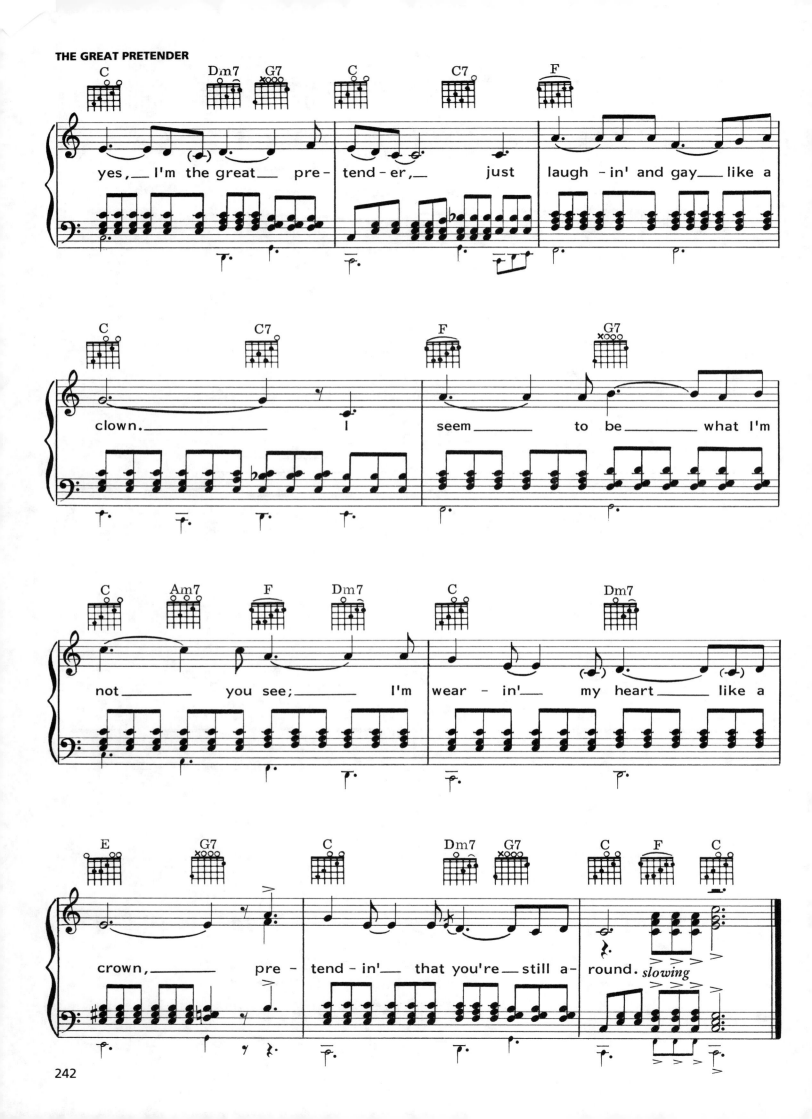

yes,__ I'm the great__ pre-tend-er,__ just laugh-in' and gay__ like a clown._____ I seem_____ to be_____ what I'm not_____ you see;_____ I'm wear-in'__ my heart_____ like a crown,_____ pre-tend-in'__ that you're__ still a-round. *slowing*

242

By 1952, when Kay Starr hit the charts with this effort by the composers of "Oh, What It Seemed to Be," "Rumors Are Flying" and "Cross Over the Bridge," she was already a major singer. She had paid her big-band dues with Glenn Miller and Charlie Barnet, among others, and recorded with such jazz greats as Benny Carter and Joe Venuti. But the Oklahoma-born singer's roots were in country music, and "Wheel of Fortune" took her right back—thereby opening the way to such further '50s hits as "Side by Side," "Changing Partners" and "Rock and Roll Waltz."

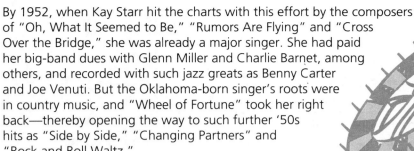

WHeeL oF FoRTUNe

Words and Music by Bennie Benjamin and George David Weiss

My Special Angel

Some people contend that Nashville's reign as a major pop hit factory began with this 1957 crossover success. Texas-born composer Jimmy Duncan had been writing songs since age 11, but "My Special Angel"—as performed by Bobby Helms—put him on the wider popular music map. The tune, which reached No. 7 in November, was one of three hits that Helms had in late '57: his recording of "Fraulein" climbed the charts in October, and the seasonal favorite "Jingle-Bell Rock" clicked in December.

Words and Music by Jimmy Duncan

sent an an-gel to love. You are my spe-cial an-gel,

right from par-a-dise; I know that you're an an-gel,

heav-en's in your eyes. A smile from your lips brings the

sum-mer sun-shine, the tears from your eyes bring the rain. I

MY SPECIAL ANGEL

They only had one hit—but it made the doo-wopping Penguins one of the most important groups in the development of rock and roll. Co-written by Penguin founder Curtis Williams, "Earth Angel" was among the first rhythm-and-blues records to make it onto the pop charts, in December 1954. A "cover" version by The Crew Cuts was also a tremendous success, but for many people The Penguins' recording will always be the definitive one. (And how many remember that "Hey Senorita" was on the other side?)

Earth Angel

Words and Music by Dootsie Williams

Slow doo-wop tempo *(with a triplet feel; ♫ played as ♩³♪)*

Earth an-gel, earth an-gel, will you be mine?__ My dar-ling dear,__ love you all the time.__ I'm just a fool,__ a fool in love with you. Earth an-gel, earth an-gel,

Sincerely

Like uncle, like nephew. Harvey Fuqua, who wrote "Sincerely" with disc jockey Alan Freed and sang it to fame with his group The Moonglows in 1954, was the nephew of Charlie Fuqua, one of the original Ink Spots. The McGuire Sisters—Chris, Dotty and Phyllis—who were then part of Arthur Godfrey's troupe, had an even bigger hit with the song, turning it into a million-seller.

Words and Music by Harvey Fuqua and Alan Freed

Slow rock and roll

Lyrics:
Sin - cere - ly, / cere - ly, oh,___ yes,___ sin -
cere - ly, / love you. oh, you know___ how I

cere - ly, / 'cause I love you so___ dear - ly.___
love you. / I'll do an - y - thing___ for___ you;

___ Please say___ you'll be mine.___ Sin -
___ Please say___ you'll be

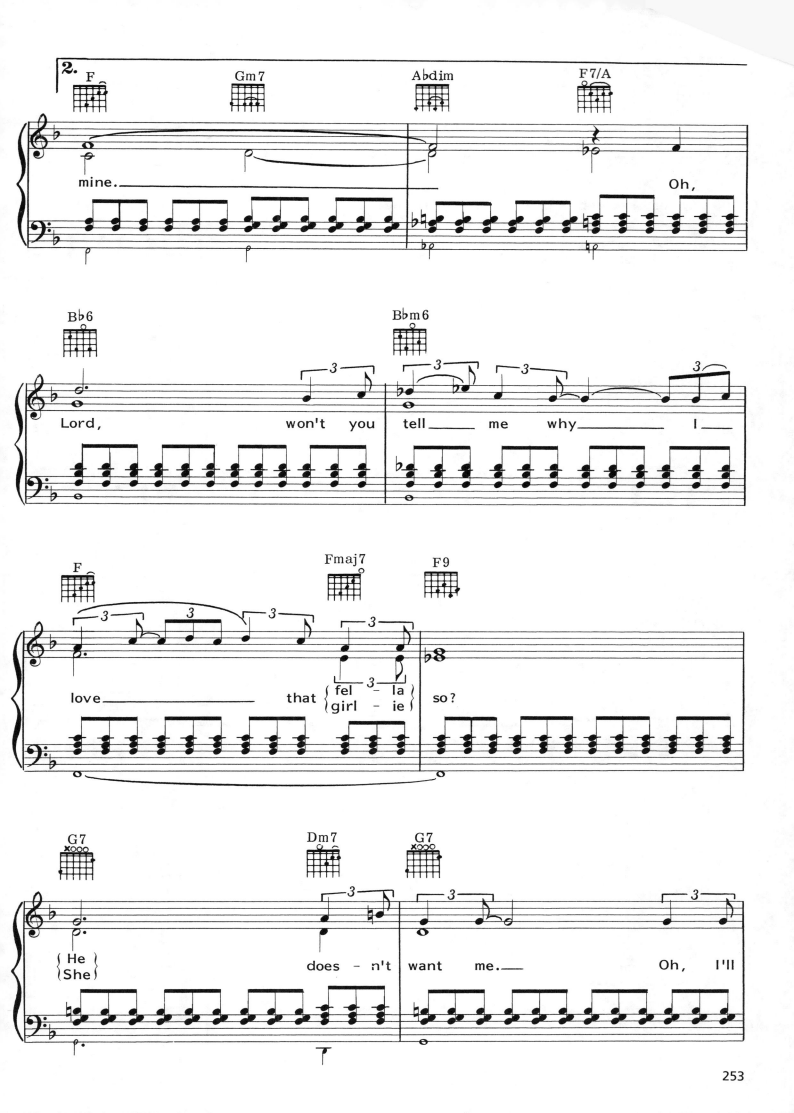

Put Your Head on My Shoulder

Paul Anka may have started out as just another teen idol in the late '50s, but he didn't let it rest there. As an actor he did well in *The Longest Day* (and wrote the title song); his translation of the French song "Comme d'Habitude" helped make "My Way" one of Frank Sinatra's greatest hits; he wrote the theme for Johnny Carson's *Tonight* show; and meanwhile he had 33 Top 40 hits between 1957 and 1983, including "Lonely Boy," "Diana" and "(You're) Having My Baby." In this 1958 ode he offered a soft-edged alternative to the rock revolution.

Words and Music by Paul Anka

Tom Dooley

His name was really Tom Dula, and he returned a hero to his hometown of Statesville, North Carolina, after fighting in the Civil War—only to walk into tragedy. Under circumstances that have never been quite clear, Tom stabbed a girlfriend to death, and died for it on the gallows. His story was recounted in a folk ballad which, adapted and toned down a bit by The Kingston Trio in 1958, became a major hit and focal point of the late '50s folk music revival.

SECTION NINE

FOLK-STYLE HITS OF THE '50S

Words and Music Collected, Adapted and Arranged by Frank Warner, John A. Lomax and Alan Lomax. From the singing of Frank Proffitt

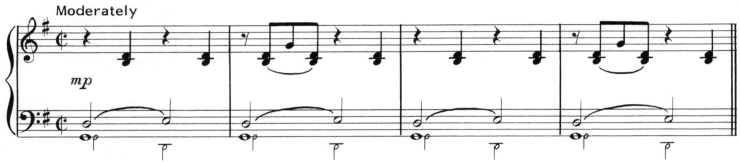

Moderately

mp

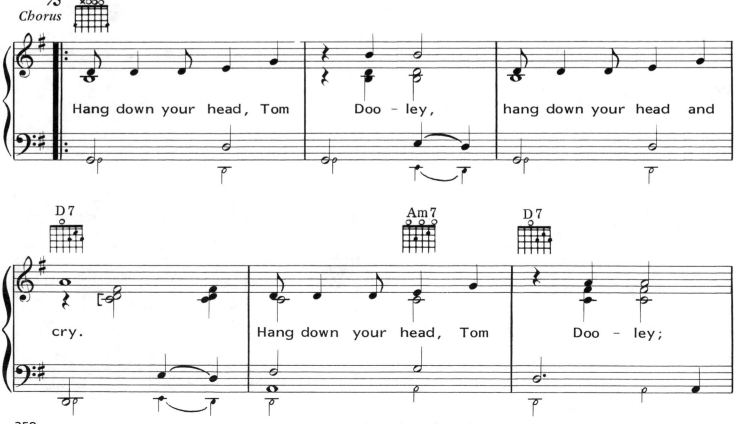

Chorus   **G**

Hang down your head, Tom Doo-ley, hang down your head and

D7   **Am7**   **D7**

cry.   Hang down your head, Tom Doo-ley;

THE TWELFTH OF NEVER

This well-traveled folk ballad probably started life in England, then showed up in the Kentucky hills as "The Riddle Song," or "I Gave My Love a Cherry." Altered a bit by Jerry Livingston and dressed up with a lyric by Paul Francis Webster, it made the charts in 1957 on the strength of a record by Johnny Mathis. Still later, such country artists as Slim Whitman "discovered" it, and the old song seems to have found a home at last as a country-folk standard.

Words by Paul Francis Webster; Music by Jerry Livingston

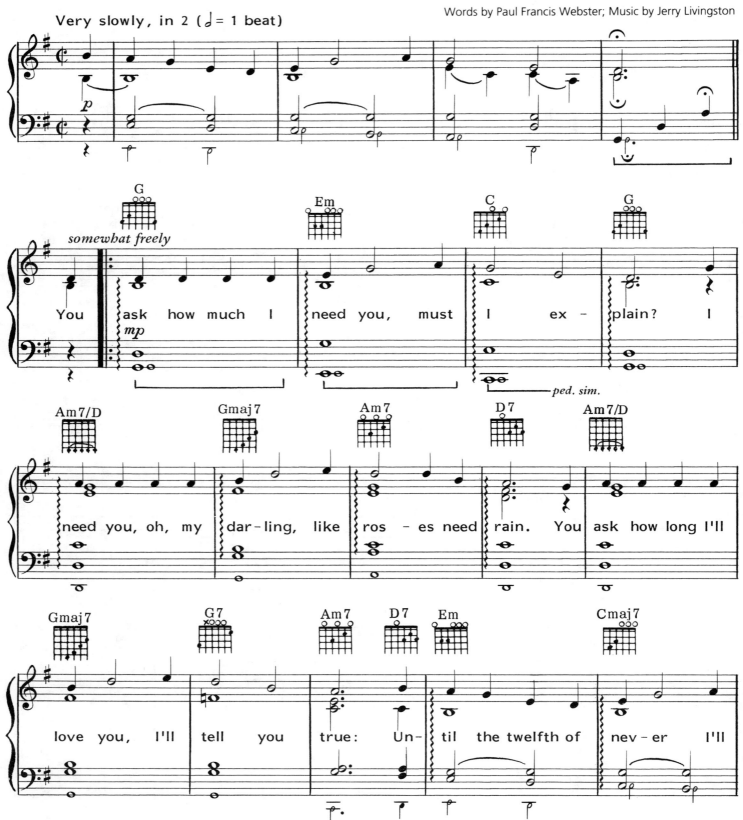

still be lov-ing you. Hold me close, nev-er let me go. Hold me close, melt my heart like A-pril snow. I'll love you till the blue-bells for-get to bloom. I'll love you till the clo-ver has

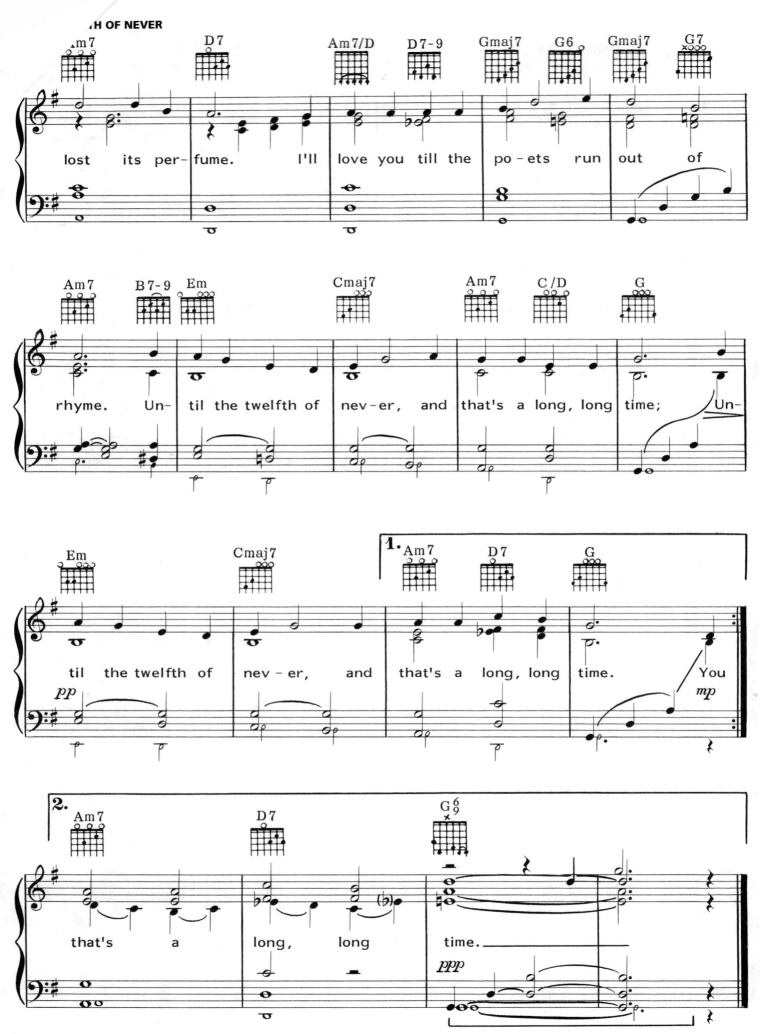

This English import became part of American history when settlers sang it while driving their covered wagons into the unexplored vastness of the West. By the early '50s, when The Weavers recorded it, the beloved folk ballad was as much a part of musical America as "The Blue-Tail Fly." The big folk music boom of the late '50s, in fact, can be traced directly to this and other old favorites put in circulation by the four singers.

On Top of Old Smokey

Moderate waltz

Traditional; arranged and adapted by Dan Fox

Lyrics:

1. 5. On top of Old Smo — key_____ all cov-ered with snow,_____ I___ lost my true lov — er_____ from___ court-in' too slow._____
2. For court-in's a plea — sure_____ but part-ing is grief,_____ and a false-heart-ed lov — er_____ is___ worse___ than a thief._____
3. A thief he will rob you_____ and take what you have,_____ but a false-heart-ed lov — er_____ will___ send you to your grave._____
4. (S)He'll hug you and kiss you_____ and tell you more lies_____ than the ties on the rail — road_____ or the stars___ in the skies._____

GOODNIGHT, IRENE

Huddie Ledbetter, best known as Leadbelly, was in every sense larger than life. Powerful of both build and temperament, he spent much of his adult years in prison—but was also a singer and 12-string guitarist of volcanic passion. He learned "Goodnight, Irene" from his uncle near the end of World War I, he said, and sang it for years. The Weavers, a quartet of white folksingers who were among his disciples, recorded it and in 1950—six months after Leadbelly's death—made it a major hit.

Moderate waltz tempo

Words and Music by Huddie Ledbetter and John Lomax

I - rene, good- night,_____ I - rene, good-

night._____ Good- night, I - rene, good- night, I - rene, I'll

see you in my dreams.____

last time slowing . . . .

Skip to verses

1. Last
2. _____
3. Stop

Final ending

dreams.____
. . . . . .

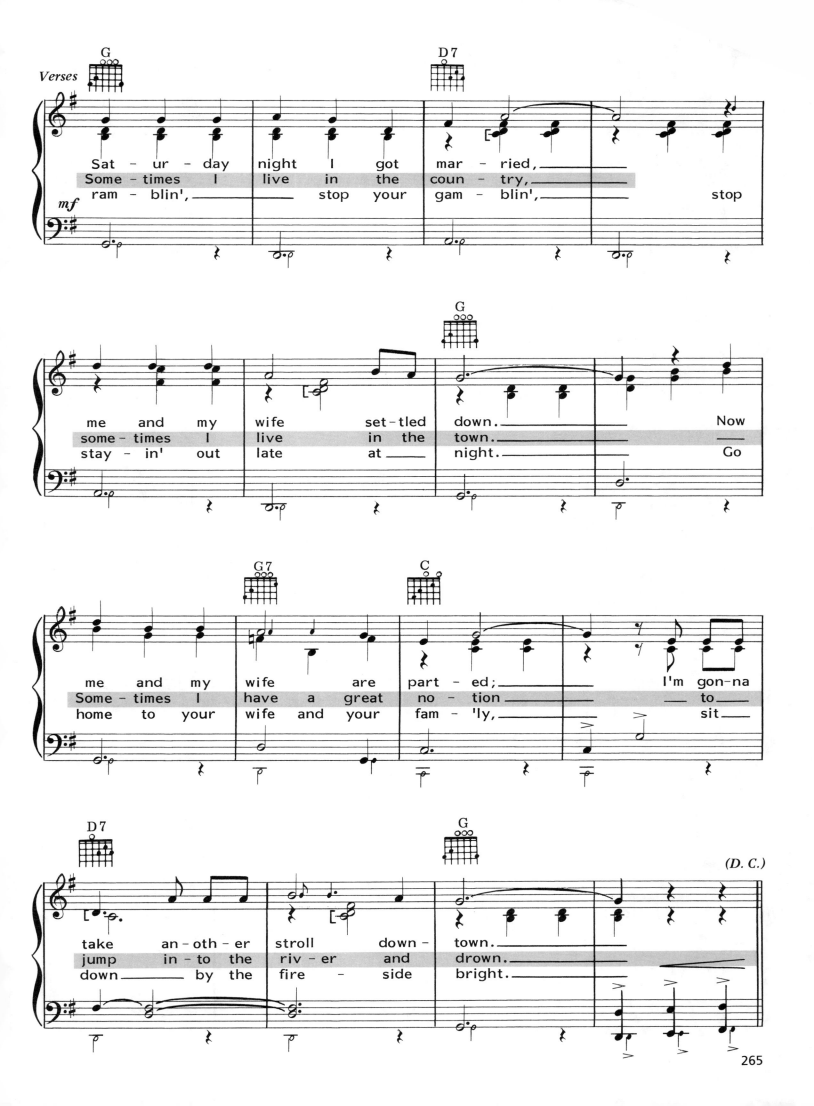

In the mid-'50s, the calypso beat danced its way up from the West Indies to the United States. One of its chief proponents was American-born, Jamaica-bred Harry Belafonte, who scored with such hits as "Jamaica Farewell" and "Banana Boat Song (Day-O)." Also along for the ride were Terry Gilkyson and The Easy Riders, who had a million-selling hit with this Bahamanian folk song in 1957. Our version features new lyrics and a musical adaptation by arranger Dan Fox and Jacquelyn Reinach.

New Words and Musical Adaptation by Jacquelyn Reinach and Dan Fox

Moderate Calypso

All day,— all night,— Mar-y Anne,—

down by— the sea-shore— sift-in' sand.— All the lit-tle

chil-dren— love Mar-y Anne,— 'cause she— can dance like—

To Verses — no one can.— 1. When 2. Then

Last time only — no one can.—

266

Kisses Sweeter Than Wine

Leadbelly and The Weavers teamed up to adapt this Irish folk song. The Weavers' record joined "On Top of Old Smokey," "So Long (It's Been Good to Know Yuh)" and "Wimoweh" among their all-time hits. But it was Jimmie Rodgers who had the big hit with "Kisses Sweeter Than Wine," in 1957. It followed his first success, "Honeycomb," in a string of hits that also included "Oh-Oh, I'm Falling in Love Again" and "Secretly."

Words by Paul Campbell; Music by Joel Newman (Pseudonymns for The Weavers and Leadbelly)

1. (He) When
2. (She) He
3. (He) I
4. (He) Our
5. (Both) ___

269

Got the Whole World in His Hands

Who can hear this old gospel favorite without remembering Mahalia Jackson singing it, majestic in her white robes, her voice ringing out triumphantly? Miss Jackson's recording made the charts in 1958, but it was a 13-year-old British singer, Laurie London, who took "He's Got the Whole World in His Hands" to No. 1 the same year.

Traditional; Adapted and Arranged by Dan Fox

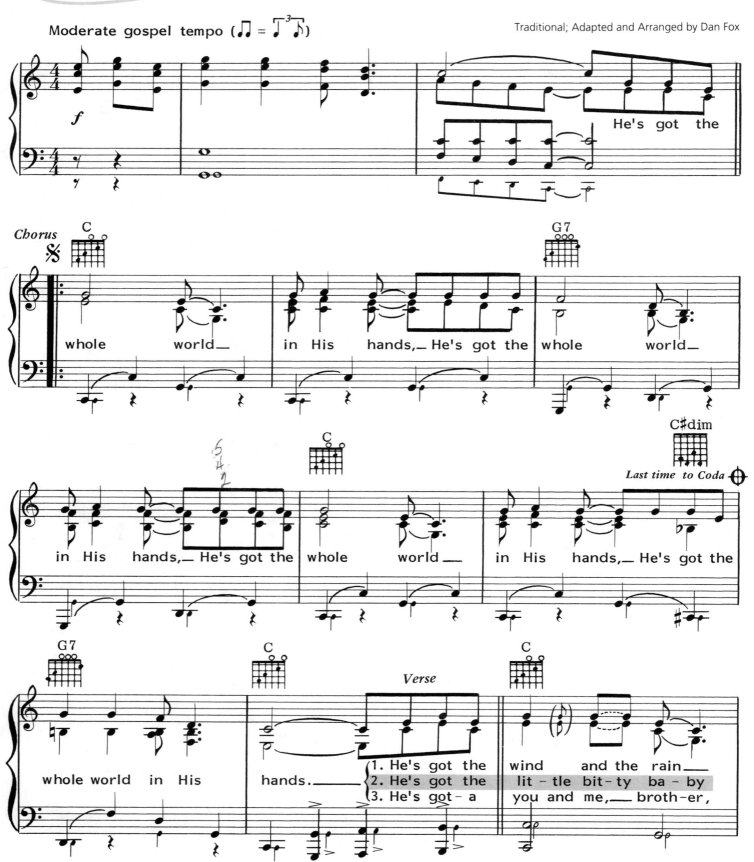

Suggestions for other verses

He's got-a you and me, sister, in His hands...

He's got the gamblin' man in His hands...

The Yellow Rose of Texas

Don George, a sometime associate of Duke Ellington, adapted this century-old Civil War song in 1955. Originally known as "The Gallant Hood of Texas," after Confederate General John Bell Hood, it was a favorite of President Franklin Roosevelt in the '30s, and was sung in a 1952 movie, *Night Stage to Galveston,* by Gene Autry. Mitch Miller's recording made the song a popular hit—and established the bearded record producer and former classical oboist as a pop star in his own right.

Bright, spirited march

Words and Music by J.K.; adapted by Don George

Chorus

if I ev – er find her, we nev – er – more will part.
prom – ised to re – turn___ and not to leave her so.   She's the
Yel – low Rose of Tex – as shall be mine for – ev – er – more.

sweet-est lit-tle rose-bud that Tex-as ev – er knew.   Her eyes are bright as

dia-monds, they spar-kle like the dew.   You may talk a-bout your

Clem – en – tine and sing of Ros – a – lee, but the Yel – low Rose of

Tex – as is the on – ly girl for me!   2. Where the   me!
3. Oh,___

Yellow Bird

Pioneer choreographer Katherine Dunham first adapted this West Indian folk melody in the '40s for use in one of her dances, titling it "Chaconne." But in 1957, choral director Norman Luboff teamed with Alan Bergman and Marilyn Keith (soon to become husband and wife) in adding a lyric and transforming it into the popular calypso-tinged song "Yellow Bird." Hit records by such artists as The Mills Brothers did the rest.

Moderate Calypso tempo

Words by Marilyn Keith and Alan Bergman; Music by Norman Luboff

Chorus

Yel - low bird, up high in ba-na-na tree,

Yel - low bird, you sit all a-lone like me.

YELLOW BIRD

276   *Repeat from the sign 𝄋 ; last time go to Fine and end there.*